The Amazing Adventures of
MR. GRANT MONEY

STRIVE press

Dear Reader,

Thank you for joining us on this exciting journey with The Amazing Adventures of Mr. Grant Money. I'm thrilled to share the valuable insights and transformative lessons within these pages —lessons that have empowered countless students, educators, and organizations to achieve remarkable success in securing scholarships and grant funding.

Scholarships and grants are powerful tools for opening doors to opportunity, and this book is designed to be your trusted companion as you navigate the intricate world of funding for education. Within these stories, you'll find not just engaging narratives but essential lessons and strategies to guide you and your students toward securing the financial support needed to achieve your academic goals.

This book is more than a collection of stories—it's part of a comprehensive approach to scholarship and grant education. As you read and engage with the exercises, I hope you discover actionable strategies and inspiration to elevate your efforts to new heights.

I'd also like to introduce you to an invaluable resource: our specially curated content on the Mr. Grant Money website. At www.mrgrantmoney.com/college-scholarships, you'll find in-depth information, book reviews, bonus content, and resources to help you go even further. This is just one book in a five-part series, each designed as part of a comprehensive curriculum that can guide you and your students through an entire year of training in grant and scholarship acquisition.

When you visit our website, be sure to check out the blog, where you'll find additional stories and articles. You'll also enjoy our deep-dive interviews and podcast-style discussions that make learning both enjoyable and engaging. For schools and organizations interested in maximizing the impact of this curriculum, I encourage you to explore our licensing program, which provides access to exclusive resources, saves time, and helps you make the most of these lessons.

Finally, because we believe learning should be both fun and memorable, don't miss the Mr. Grant Money music collection—a perfect complement to this educational journey. With its upbeat tracks and inspirational messages, the music is a great way to enhance the learning experience for you and your students. Explore more at www.mrgrantmoney.com/music.
Thank you for allowing The Amazing Adventures of Mr. Grant Money to be a part of your educational journey. Together, let's unlock the doors to opportunity and success!

Best Regards,

Rodney
Grant Central USA

P.S. Be sure to visit our website and sign up for our newsletters to stay current.

The Amazing Adventures of
MR. GRANT MONEY

Scholarship Odyssey:
Mr. Grant Money's Roadmap

VOLUME ONE

RODNEY WALKER

Chief Editor: Laine Minerales
Editorial Assistant: Daniel Tuano
Production Supervisor: Joerje Galo
Electronic Composition: Jairus Agoncillo
Photographer: Studio 5404
Executive Marketing Manager: Jimmy Moore

Discover the breadth of our series, encompassing a myriad of crucial topics. Delve into the realms of grant acquisition, college scholarships, entrepreneurship, social impact, philanthropy, and beyond. Unearth a treasure trove of knowledge and empowerment within our diverse collection. Explore the wealth of insights awaiting you across these transformative series.

To inquire about utilizing The Amazing Adventures of Mr. Grant Money books in the classroom, securing licensing, and exploring special pricing for bulk orders, kindly contact us at info@grantcentralusa.com.

ISBN: 979-8-89725-026-4 (Hardback)
ISBN: 979-8-89725-000-4 (Paperback)
ISBN: 979-8-89725-029-5 (Ebook)
ISBN: 979-8-89725-038-7 (Audiobook)

Printed in the United States

Dedication

This book is dedicated to every young dreamer who's ever been overlooked, underestimated, or told their goals were out of reach. To the underdogs who face doubts from others—and sometimes even themselves—know this: your potential is limitless, your voice matters, and your future is yours to create.

Go prove the doubters wrong, surpass every expectation, and build a life so extraordinary that even you will stand in awe. I'm cheering for you every step of the way. Believe in yourself, because I already do. You've got this!

With sincere appreciation,

Rodney

PREFACE

I will never forget the day I walked into my high school guidance counselor's office, eager to embrace the challenge of honors English. The summer had been spent in a relentless pursuit of knowledge, and I believed I was ready to take on the academic challenges that awaited me. Little did I know that this simple request would set the stage for a pivotal moment that would shape my trajectory through my senior year and beyond.

My counselor, perhaps fueled by a misguided notion, walked me down the hallway and gestured towards a nearly all-white honors English classroom. With a pointed question, she challenged my ability to compete with the students within. In that moment, my confidence wavered, and the doubt crept in. As a senior in my final year of high school, the seed of uncertainty took root. If my counselor questioned my readiness, maybe I wasn't up to the challenge.

Regrettably, I succumbed to that doubt and chose not to enroll in honors English. It marked the beginning of a phase where I stopped giving my best and started coasting through the remainder of my senior year, doing just enough to get by. Little did I realize the impact this decision would have on my direct path to the college of my choice. While I did eventually find my way to that desired college, the journey was not straightforward. I was uninformed about the college application process, and the entire endeavor felt like a maze with no guide to lead me through. I vividly remember the moment of embarrassment when a peer proudly announced her chosen college, and I found myself unable to answer the same question because I hadn't even applied.

It was this moment of realization, coupled with my own winding journey to college and later earning a Master's in Business Administration, that fueled a promise to myself. I vowed that when the time was right, I would do my part to help others navigate the complex terrain of college admissions and secure scholarships for a brighter future.

This book is the fulfillment of that promise.

While there are countless books on scholarships and navigating the college landscape, I wanted to offer something different. Inspired by my own experiences, I sought to create a book that not only imparts practical knowledge but also inspires young readers to dream bigger. I want to encourage them with stories that stretch the imagination and showcase the boundless possibilities that education and perseverance can unlock.

As I reflect on that fateful day in the hallway, where uncertainty and embarrassment loomed large, I am grateful for the counselor whose words became the catalyst for this journey. In many ways, her doubts became the fuel that propelled me to excel, and now, with this book, I am committed to providing the guidance and inspiration I wish I had received.

To every young mind yearning for knowledge, every dreamer aspiring to greatness, and every individual navigating the intricate path to higher education, may this book be a beacon of hope and a source of invaluable scholarship success secrets.

With determination and dedication,

Rodney Walker

TABLE OF CONTENT

Introduction   8

Beyond Grants: The Scholarship Chronicles   9

Scholarship Symphony: Scholarly Serendipity at Mrs. Universe   16

Fast-Track Scholarships: Mr. Grant Money's Need for Speed   23

Beyond Boundaries: The Symphony of Mr. Grant Money's Guidance   30

Scholarly Soiree: Mr. Grant Money's High-Flying Scholarly Sojourn   37

Dreams, Scepters, and Scholarship Super Bowls   44

Emerald City Insights: Scholarships and STEM Dreams   51

Big Easy Rhythms: Scholarship Jazz in New Orleans   58

Beyond the Nap: A Butterfly's Gift of Collective Scholarship Mastery   65

The Celestial Gala Chronicles: Mr. Grant Money's Odyssey to Cosmic Wisdom   72

Afterward   79

About the Author   80

INTRODUCTION

Embark on a transformative voyage through the realms of academia with "The Adventures of Mr. Grant Money: A Scholarship Odyssey." This remarkable literary gem defies conventional scholarship guides, inviting you into a captivating narrative where the pursuit of financial aid becomes an exhilarating journey filled with unexpected twists, turns, and triumphant revelations.

In this unparalleled odyssey, Mr. Grant Money isn't just a mentor; he's a charismatic guide leading you through the labyrinth of scholarships with infectious enthusiasm and a dash of wit. Brace yourself for an extraordinary reading experience as this book seamlessly weaves essential strategies, practical tips, and entertaining anecdotes, ensuring that the pursuit of scholarships becomes not only an educational endeavor but an enjoyable adventure.

Gone are the days of monotonous advice and dry application protocols. Mr. Grant Money breathes life into the scholarship process, narrating tales of successful applications with a zest that transforms you from a passive reader into an active participant in your scholarship journey. Prepare to unlock the art of scholarship pursuit and discover innovative approaches and winning strategies that will set you on the path to academic triumph.

"The Adventures of Mr. Grant Money" stands out not just for its engaging storytelling but also for its meticulous design. Dive into thought-provoking discussion questions, engage in practical application through actionable exercises, add a playful twist with word searches, find inspiration in big ideas, and draw motivation from poignant quotes. This book isn't just a guide; it's a comprehensive toolkit for success.

What sets this odyssey apart is the unwavering commitment to ensuring that you don't merely acquire knowledge but revel in the learning process. Mr. Grant Money speaks directly to you, bridging the gap between advice and enjoyment. The book's strategic design aims to keep you hooked, eagerly turning each page in anticipation of uncovering the secrets that will pave the way to scholarship success.

As you embark on this literary expedition, prepare to experience the thrill of scholarship conquest. "The Adventures of Mr. Grant Money" is more than just a book; it's a transformative journey that promises not only to educate but to empower. **Get ready to enjoy the benefits of scholarship enlightenment, empowerment, and inspiration – because your scholarship odyssey starts here.**

Beyond Grants: The Scholarship Chronicles

Discover The Untold Story Of David's Triumph And The Ripple Effect Of Scholarship Success Orchestrated By Mr. Grant Money

In an upscale Chicago office, Mr. Grant Money, the Master Grant Acquisition Specialist, sat behind his mahogany desk, dressed to the nines as always. He was a man of sharp style, known for his impeccable suits and polished shoes. On this particular day, he wore a charcoal gray suit with a crisp white shirt, a burgundy tie adding a touch of elegance. Mr. Grant Money had an air of gravitas about him, and his office, located in a high-rise building, reflected his success.

As he pondered the reports on his desk, an idea began to form in his mind. This was not the first time he had thought about helping students secure grant money, but today, the urge was more intense than ever. He couldn't ignore it any longer.

With a flash of inspiration, he reached for his special scepter, a unique object he secretly called "Shirley Scepter." It was a symbol of his dedication to helping students and organizations secure the funding they needed to achieve their dreams. As he held it in his hand, he felt a surge of determination and a sense of purpose.

A few minutes later, Mr. Grant Money's phone rang. It was a persistent teacher who had been trying to reach him for months. She had seen him on a television show, where he had shared his expertise in helping organizations secure over half a billion in grants. The teacher believed that if he could help organizations, he could certainly help their students secure scholarships.

The timing of the call seemed more than just a coincidence. Mr. Grant Money knew he couldn't ignore the universe's nudge any longer. He decided to answer the call and listen to the teacher's plea.

The teacher, Ms. Johnson, shared her vision of helping students achieve their dreams through scholarships. She had witnessed the incredible impact of scholarships on the lives of her students, and she believed that with Mr. Grant Money's guidance, they could unlock a world of opportunities.

Mr. Grant Money was initially busy with his ongoing projects, but as he spoke with Ms. Johnson, he couldn't help but envision a way to make a difference. Their shared dedication to helping students win scholarships became a powerful catalyst for change.

Together, they embarked on a journey to help a student named David. David had a dream of pursuing a college education but lacked the financial means to do so. His story was a testament to resilience, ambition, and untapped potential.

With Mr. Grant Money's expertise and Ms. Johnson's dedication, they guided David through the scholarship application process. They helped him craft compelling essays, prepare for interviews, and identify scholarship opportunities that aligned with his goals.

David's journey was not just about securing a scholarship; it was about transforming his life. With the financial support he received, he pursued his dreams, earned his degree, and went on to make a significant impact in his community.

"The Ripple Effect: David's Scholarship Success" became a symbol of the enduring impact of scholarships. David's journey inspired those around him to strive for their dreams, creating a ripple effect of success and change that extended far beyond his own achievements.

In Mr. Grant Money's Chicago office, where the idea had first sparked, the sense of fulfillment and purpose was palpable. He knew that his dedication to helping students secure grant money was not just a profession but a calling, and the lives he touched would continue to create lasting change in their communities and the world.

Exercise: "Craft Your Scholarship Success Blueprint"

Objective: Develop a personalized plan to pursue scholarship opportunities, inspired by the impactful collaboration between Mr. Grant Money, Ms. Johnson, and student David.

Steps:

1. Self-Reflection:
- Reflect on your educational and career goals. Consider the financial barriers or challenges that scholarships could help you overcome. Identify your strengths, achievements, and aspirations.

2. Research Scholarship Opportunities:
- Utilize online resources, scholarship databases, and your educational institution's resources to research potential scholarship opportunities. Look for scholarships that align with your field of study, interests, and personal background.

3. Define Your Narrative:
- Craft a personal narrative that highlights your journey, ambitions, and the impact receiving a scholarship would have on your educational and career aspirations. Develop a compelling story that sets you apart from other applicants.

4. Create a Scholarship Calendar:
- Develop a calendar that includes application deadlines, required documents, and key milestones in the scholarship application process. Organize the information to ensure you stay on track and meet all submission deadlines.

"In the symphony of life, scholarships are the notes that compose a melody of dreams. Each student we help is a key signature, and together, we create a harmonious tune that resonates with the rhythm of success."

- Mr. Grant Money

5. Identify Support Systems:

- Identify individuals who can support you in your scholarship journey. This could include teachers, mentors, or peers who can provide guidance, feedback, and encouragement. Share your goals with them and seek their assistance when needed.

6. Prepare Application Materials:

- Prepare the necessary materials for scholarship applications, including essays, recommendation letters, and resumes. Tailor each application to the specific requirements of the scholarship and showcase your unique qualities and achievements.

7. Seek Guidance from Educational Advisors:

- Schedule meetings with educational advisors or counselors who can provide insights into scholarship opportunities, application strategies, and potential sources of financial aid. Utilize their expertise to enhance your scholarship pursuit.

8. Engage in Extracurricular Activities:

- Participate in extracurricular activities that align with your interests and goals. Many scholarships consider involvement in community service, leadership roles, or specialized skills. Showcase these activities in your applications

9. Participate in Scholarship Workshops:

- Attend scholarship workshops or webinars offered by educational institutions or community organizations. These sessions often provide valuable tips, resources, and insights into the scholarship application process.

10. Stay Resilient and Adaptive:

- Understand that the scholarship application process may be competitive, and setbacks may occur. Develop a mindset of resilience, learn from experiences, and adapt your approach as needed. Stay focused on your goals.

Remember, your scholarship journey is a unique and transformative process. By crafting a personalized plan and drawing inspiration from David's success, you can embark on a path towards achieving your educational dreams.

"The Shirley Scepter isn't just a prop; it's a wand of possibilities, turning the pages of potential into the chapters of success. Every student's story written with its magic is a testament to the transformative power of belief and support."

- Mr. Grant Money

Discussion Questions

1. What role does style and presentation play in Mr. Grant Money's success? How does his impeccable attire contribute to his professional image and impact his ability to make a difference in the world of grant acquisition?

2. The story introduces the concept of the "Shirley Scepter" as a symbol of dedication and purpose. What symbolic objects or rituals do you think individuals might create in their own lives to represent their commitment to a cause or goal?

3. Discuss the significance of the teacher, Ms. Johnson, reaching out persistently to Mr. Grant Money. How does her determination to connect with him reflect the importance of pursuing opportunities and seeking guidance in achieving goals?

4. Reflect on the idea of a "Ripple Effect" in the context of David's scholarship success. How do individual achievements have the power to inspire and create positive change within communities and beyond?

5. If you were to embark on a similar journey to Mr. Grant Money, what cause or mission would you dedicate yourself to? How would you go about making a tangible impact, and what challenges might you anticipate?

Feel free to share your thoughts on any of these questions or dive deeper into specific aspects of the story that resonated with you!

 Big Idea "Personalized Success Journals"

Following David's transformative journey, create a personalized success journal for yourself. Document your goals, aspirations, and the steps you're taking to achieve them. Much like Mr. Grant Money's determination and David's resilience, use the success journal to track your progress, celebrate achievements, and learn from challenges. This practical tool can serve as a source of motivation, helping you stay focused on your dreams and the positive impact you aim to make. It's a simple yet powerful way to turn inspiration from stories like David's into actionable steps for your own success.

🔍 Word Search

Welcome to the "Mr. Grant Money Wordsearch Puzzle"! Immerse yourself in the world of grant acquisition and scholarship success as you search for key words related to Mr. Grant Money's inspiring journey. Each word is a piece of the puzzle that reflects the determination, inspiration, and impact found in the amazing story of transforming lives through education and grants.

Enjoy the challenge and discover the hidden words that echo the spirit of Mr. Grant Money's commitment to making a difference:

Now, here are the 15 words for the word search puzzle based on the story:

F	P	O	Y	A	M	B	I	T	I	O	N	S	E
P	M	R	O	F	S	N	A	R	T	R	N	A	I
R	M	G	U	I	D	A	N	C	E	O	S	P	H
M	C	S	P	P	U	R	P	O	S	E	M	R	L
M	A	R	E	S	I	L	I	E	N	C	E	D	H
D	C	I	A	O	P	E	S	C	E	P	T	E	R
G	C	I	M	P	A	C	T	D	I	V	A	D	S
F	U	L	F	I	L	L	M	E	N	T	A	P	U
T	I	U	T	T	T	G	E	P	O	O	P	E	C
E	O	D	R	A	D	A	H	L	T	N	I	I	C
H	C	H	I	C	A	G	O	C	P	P	E	N	E
N	C	O	M	M	U	N	I	T	Y	P	U	C	S
S	C	H	O	L	A	R	S	H	I	P	I	S	S
R	F	U	N	D	I	N	G	E	T	T	U	R	U

FULFILLMENT
PURPOSE
RIPPLE
TRANSFORM
GUIDANCE
COMMUNITY
DAVID
SCEPTER
AMBITION
FUNDING
SCHOLARSHIP
SUCCESS
RESILIENCE
IMPACT
CHICAGO

-CHICAGO-

"Success isn't measured by what we gain individually, but by the ripples of positive change we create together. David's scholarship success isn't just a personal achievement; it's a shared victory that elevates our entire community."

SUCCESS STORIES

"Pioneering Biomedical Engineer on a Global Stage"

In the heart of Houston, where dreams intertwine with the city skyline, Aisha Patel's story stands as a testament to the transformative power of passion, resilience, and innovation. A first-generation American, born to Indian immigrant parents, Aisha's journey from the vibrant streets of Houston to the hallowed halls of MIT is a saga of triumph against the odds.

From a young age, Aisha's fascination with the intricate complexities of the human body fueled her curiosity. Despite financial constraints and the pressure of being the first in her family to pursue higher education, she emerged as a beacon of determination. Her parents worked tirelessly, piecing together every resource, ensuring that Aisha's dreams would not be hindered by the financial labyrinth that often confronts aspiring students.

Aisha's journey wasn't a solitary climb; rather, it was a community effort. Inspired by her roots, she delved into her cultural heritage to develop an affordable medical device tailored for resource-limited communities. Her evenings were spent in makeshift laboratories, her commitment unwavering even when faced with setbacks. She leveraged her cultural background, collaborating with mentors and engineers to create a device that could potentially change lives.

It was this very commitment that caught the attention of MIT's scholarship committee. Aisha's groundbreaking research not only showcased her academic prowess but also highlighted her dedication to bridging the healthcare gap. MIT recognized in her a future pioneer, and with a full scholarship, Aisha found herself at the epicenter of technological innovation.

In a statement that resonates with both humility and determination, Aisha Patel remarked, "My journey is a testament to the power of dreams nurtured by family, community, and an unyielding passion for change. MIT has provided me with the platform to turn those dreams into reality, and I am ready to take on the challenge of shaping a better future through biomedical engineering."

Aisha's story reverberates far beyond the Houston skyline, inspiring students from diverse backgrounds to defy expectations and pursue their passions. It is a tale that whispers to every aspiring scientist, engineer, and dreamer, urging them to believe that the pursuit of knowledge knows no boundaries. As Aisha Patel takes her place at MIT, she carries with her not only the hopes of her family but also the dreams of a generation eager to embrace the limitless possibilities of education.

SCHOLARSHIP SYMPHONY

The Amazing Adventures of
MR GRANT MONEY

Scholarship Symphony: Scholarly Serendipity at Mrs. Universe

A Mischievous Parrot, A Golden Journal, And A Tale Of Scholarship Success That Echoes Beyond The Stage.

Mr. Grant Money found himself stylish as ever at the Mrs. Universe competition, an event known for its glitz and glamour. He was dressed to impress, wearing a classic midnight blue tuxedo with a crisp white shirt, a deep black silk bowtie adding a touch of elegance. His shoes gleamed, and his black and silver trimmed cufflinks subtly reflected the spotlight's glow. Mr. Grant Money had a way of blending sophistication with a hint of charisma, making him a distinguished presence wherever he went.

The Mrs. Universe competition took place in a cool and exotic location, with the stage set against a backdrop of lush palm trees and a breathtaking ocean view. As he mingled with the audience, something interesting and amusing happened. A mischievous parrot perched on a nearby branch decided to play a game of mimicry with Mr. Grant Money, much to the amusement of the onlookers.

After this charming yet unexpected encounter, Mr. Grant Money continued his exploration of the event. As he wandered behind the scenes, he found himself granted special access to the contestants. He overheard a conversation among three young ladies who were intently listening to one contestant, Olivia, as she shared her story of winning multiple grants and the profound impact they had on her life.

Olivia was a poised and articulate contestant, and her voice carried the weight of sincerity. She spoke of the grants she had won and how they had helped relieve a substantial financial burden. She had managed to secure funds that allowed her to pursue her education and chase her dreams.

Mr. Grant Money couldn't help but listen in on Olivia's conversation, as her words resonated deeply with his own mission to help students secure grant money.

Olivia shared some practical insights into her scholarship success:

1. Diversity of Applications: She explained that she applied to a wide range of scholarships, each tailored to her specific talents, achievements, and goals. By diversifying her applications, she maximized her chances of winning.

2. Customized Essays: Olivia described how she spent considerable time customizing her scholarship essays for each application. She highlighted her unique experiences and how they aligned with the scholarship's mission and values.

3. Recommendation Letters: She emphasized the importance of strong recommendation letters from teachers and mentors who knew her well. These letters painted a vivid picture of her character and accomplishments.

4. Consistent Effort: Olivia revealed that winning scholarships required consistent effort. She applied to multiple scholarships, continuously improved her essays, and sought feedback from teachers and peers to enhance her applications.

Mr. Grant Money discreetly noted down Olivia's insights in his Golden Journal, his scepter of wisdom in hand. He realized that her practical approach to winning scholarships was a valuable lesson to share with students everywhere.

Olivia's journey was a testament to the transformative power of securing grants and scholarships. Her dedication and strategic approach had not only relieved her financial burden but also opened doors to a brighter future. And for Mr. Grant Money, her story added a new dimension to his mission – to gather practical insights and share them with students worldwide, helping them achieve their dreams and lessen the burden of educational expenses.

Exercise: "Scholarship Strategy Blueprint"

By following this exercise, you'll develop a strategic approach to scholarship applications, maximizing your chances of securing financial support for your education. Remember, consistency, customization, and a thoughtful strategy can significantly impact your success in the competitive world of scholarships.

Steps:

1. Identify Your Strengths and Goals:
- Take some time to reflect on your strengths, achievements, and long-term goals. Consider what makes you unique and how your aspirations align with your chosen field of study.

2. Research Diverse Scholarships:
- Explore a variety of scholarships that cater to different aspects of your profile, such as academic achievements, extracurricular activities, community service, or specific talents. Look beyond the obvious and find opportunities that resonate with your individuality.

3. Create a Customized List:
- Develop a list of scholarships you plan to apply for, ensuring that each one aligns with specific aspects of your profile. Include a mix of local, national, and niche scholarships to maximize your chances of success.

4. Craft Tailored Essays:
- For each scholarship on your list, invest time in crafting personalized essays. Highlight your unique experiences, achievements, and how they relate to the scholarship's mission and values. Tailor each essay to address the specific criteria outlined by the scholarship providers.

"In the symphony of opportunity, the notes of perseverance, diversity, and passion compose the melody of scholarship success. Each application, a unique instrument, contributes to the harmonious composition of one's educational journey."

- Mr. Grant Money

5. Build Strong Relationships for Recommendations:
- Identify teachers, mentors, or individuals who know you well and can provide compelling recommendation letters. Approach them early, share your scholarship goals, and provide them with the necessary information to write detailed and authentic letters on your behalf.

6. Establish a Consistent Application Schedule:
- Create a timeline for submitting your scholarship applications. Break down the process into manageable steps, setting aside dedicated time each week for research, essay writing, and application submission. Consistency is key to increasing your chances of success.

7. Seek Feedback and Continuous Improvement:
- Share your scholarship essays with teachers, mentors, or peers who can provide constructive feedback. Use this input to continuously improve and refine your applications. Embrace the mindset of constant refinement to enhance the quality of your submissions.

8. Document Your Progress:
- Keep a journal or document your scholarship application journey. Record the scholarships you've applied to, the feedback received, and any notable achievements or challenges. This documentation can serve as a valuable reference for future applications.

> *"As the parrot mimics the echoes of the crowd, so should we mirror the qualities that resonate with scholarship providers—authenticity, dedication, and a touch of charm. The song of success begins with the dance of genuine effort and the rhythm of strategic persistence."*
>
> *- Mr. Grant Money*

Discussion Questions

1. Mr. Grant Money's style and charisma made him stand out at the Mrs. Universe competition. How do you believe personal presentation and charisma can impact one's presence in different settings, and what role do you think it plays in achieving personal and professional goals? Share instances where you've witnessed the influence of presentation and charisma in real-life situations.

2. The mischievous parrot's game of mimicry added an unexpected twist to the event. If you were organizing a unique and memorable event, what unexpected element would you introduce to make it stand out and create lasting memories for the attendees? Discuss how such unexpected elements contribute to the overall experience of an event.

3. Olivia's story highlights the transformative power of winning grants. How do you think financial assistance can contribute to personal and educational growth? Share your thoughts on the long-term impact of securing funds for pursuing one's dreams and aspirations.

4. Olivia's success in securing scholarships is attributed to a strategic approach. Which of the practical insights shared by Olivia do you find most valuable, and how do you think it can be applied to enhance your own educational or career pursuits? Share specific examples or experiences that align with Olivia's strategies.

5. Mr. Grant Money's mission is to share practical insights with students worldwide. How can the collective sharing of practical experiences and wisdom contribute to a more informed and empowered student community? Discuss the potential benefits of creating a platform for students to share their insights and lessons learned in navigating educational challenges.

 ## Big Idea "The Global Scholarship Hub"

Create an online platform, "The Global Scholarship Hub," that serves as a comprehensive resource for students seeking scholarships. The platform would feature a user-friendly interface with detailed information on a wide array of scholarships, categorized based on different criteria such as academic achievements, talents, and goals. Users can create personalized profiles, allowing the platform to recommend tailored scholarship opportunities. Additionally, the hub could provide a database of sample customized essays, guidance on securing strong recommendation letters, and tips on maintaining consistent effort in the application process. This platform aims to empower students globally by centralizing practical insights and resources, making the scholarship application journey more accessible and efficient.

🔍 Word Search

Welcome to the "Mr. Grant Money Wordsearch Puzzle," where the glitz and glamour of the Mrs. Universe competition meet the wisdom of Mr. Grant Money. Explore the stylish world of scholarships as you search for key words inspired by the elegant journey of Mr. Grant Money and the transformative stories of Olivia.

Each hidden word carries the essence of scholarship success, from diversity and customized essays to recommendation letters and consistent effort. Can you uncover the golden words that pave the way to educational dreams? Let the search begin!

Now, here are the 14 words for the word search puzzle based on the story:

C	T	N	R	C	L	R	N	F	F	D	E	U	S
H	R	H	A	C	R	M	O	O	I	I	T	O	K
A	A	P	R	R	D	N	I	I	L	V	O	P	N
R	N	I	E	A	S	A	S	M	I	E	R	I	I
I	S	H	A	A	L	R	S	O	P	R	R	N	L
S	F	S	L	H	E	I	I	D	P	S	A	A	F
M	O	R	A	G	E	E	M	S	A	I	P	E	F
A	R	A	N	O	O	L	A	I	T	T	S	C	U
V	M	L	R	L	R	L	E	W	O	Y	V	O	C
P	A	O	U	D	E	R	I	G	F	P	F	I	R
S	T	H	O	E	I	C	I	V	A	E	E	N	E
C	I	C	J	N	P	R	P	S	I	N	P	S	H
E	V	S	C	T	E	M	S	P	N	A	C	S	S
N	E	G	F	S	H	E	F	F	O	R	T	E	R

OCEAN
OLIVIA
MISSION
ELEGANCE
DIVERSITY
TRANSFORMATIVE
SCHOLARSHIP
CUFFLINKS
EFFORT
WISDOM
CHARISMA
GOLDEN
PARROT
JOURNAL

"The journey from financial burden to open doors is crafted with the keys of diversity, personalized narratives, and resonant letters. Scholarships, like a map, guide us to the landscapes of knowledge, shaping dreams into tangible realities."

SUCCESS STORIES

"Jamal Williams: Coding a Future Beyond Boundaries"

In the heart of Detroit, amidst the echoes of a city's resilience, Jamal Williams, a young African American with an unwavering determination, has forged a path that transcends socioeconomic constraints, proving that brilliance knows no zip code.

Growing up in a neighborhood where opportunities were scarce and adversity abundant, Jamal found solace in the world of computers. His humble surroundings echoed with the rhythmic tap of his fingers against the keys, each keystroke a step towards a brighter future. Despite financial hardships, Jamal's parents recognized his potential and scraped together enough to provide him with a secondhand laptop.

Jamal's educational journey was marked by a relentless pursuit of knowledge. With limited access to advanced courses, he turned to online resources, teaching himself the intricacies of coding and software development. His passion found an outlet in an innovative app designed to address local community issues. The app not only tackled problems but also empowered residents by providing a platform for community engagement and education.

Word of Jamal's app spread, and soon he found himself presenting it at local tech events. However, his aspirations reached far beyond Detroit's city limits. Undeterred by the challenges, Jamal applied for scholarships, showcasing not only his technical skills but also his commitment to community empowerment.

The acceptance letter from Stanford was more than a ticket to higher education; it was a validation of Jamal's resilience and an acknowledgment that talent, when nurtured, knows no racial or economic boundaries. In a press release, Jamal shared, "Coding became my passport to a world of endless possibilities. Stanford is not just a university; it's a gateway to turn my dreams into code, to make a real impact on communities around the world."

Jamal Williams' story isn't just about overcoming financial barriers; it's a narrative of leveraging technology for social change. His journey serves as a beacon to aspiring programmers in underserved communities, illustrating that with a laptop, determination, and a bit of code, one can break through the constraints that society imposes.

As Jamal embarks on his Stanford adventure, he carries with him the hopes of a community that believes in the transformative power of education. His story is a reminder that innovation knows no boundaries, and with the right support, a brilliant mind can emerge from the most unexpected corners of our cities, ready to code a future that transcends limitations.

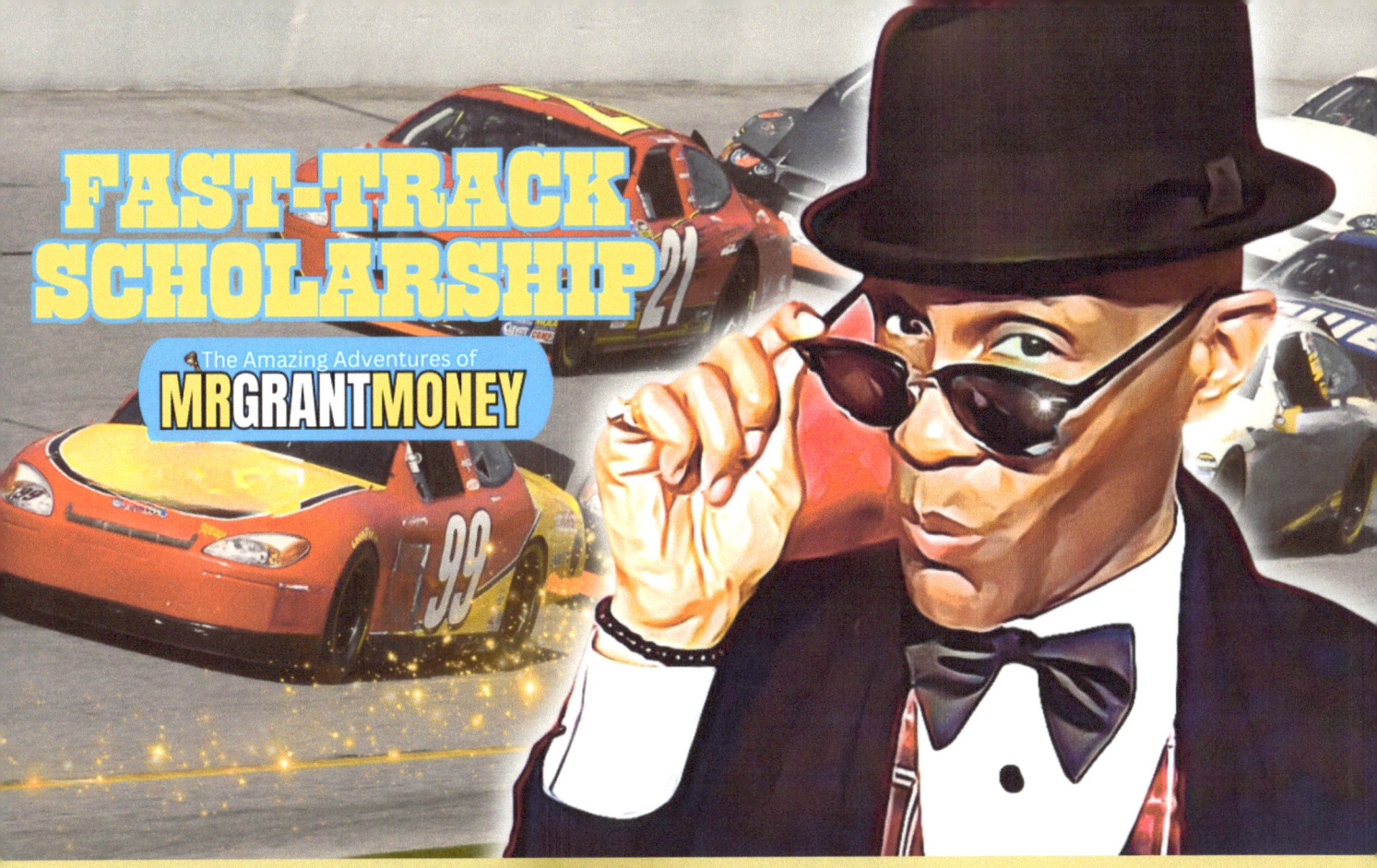

Fast-Track Scholarships: Mr. Grant Money's Need for Speed

Unleash The Velocity Of Opportunities – Apply Widely, Apply Promptly!

Mr. Grant Money's adventures took an unexpected turn when he won a special prize from a silent auction. The grand prize gave him the opportunity to drive at high speeds for several exhilarating laps at the iconic Indy 500, just a few days before the big event. Dressed as stylishly as ever, he donned a sleek racing jumpsuit and helmet, ready to hit the tracks.

As he revved up the engine and zoomed down the straightaways, Mr. Grant Money couldn't help but feel the rush of excitement. He drove with the grace of international roadster but with a unique flair that was even cooler. The wind grazed across his helmet, and the world became a blur of speed and adrenaline.

In the midst of this thrilling experience, he made a parallel with driving fast and applying fast to diverse places to win as many opportunities as possible. The engine's roar became a metaphor for the pace of life, and Mr. Grant Money's mind raced with thoughts on how to share this wisdom with young people.

Thinking to himself, he came up with a powerful quote: "Life is a fast track, and to secure your dreams, you need to apply fast and apply widely."

This quote encapsulated the essence of his mission. Just as he had learned from Olivia about diversifying scholarship applications, Mr. Grant Money realized that the key to success was to cast a wide net, apply to diverse opportunities, and apply promptly.

Back in his office, he devised a way to share these practical insights with more young people. He created an interactive online platform that offered a wealth of resources, including scholarship directories, application tips, and guidance on applying to diverse grants and scholarships. He wanted to make the path to securing grant money as fast and efficient as a high-speed race.

The takeaways were clear:

1. **Diversity of Applications**: Apply for a wide range of opportunities that match your unique skills, experiences, and goals.

2. **Customize Your Applications**: Tailor your essays and documents to each application to demonstrate a strong alignment with the scholarship's mission and values.

3. **Apply Promptly**: Don't wait. Apply as soon as you find a suitable scholarship or grant opportunity. Speed can make a difference.

4. **Persevere**: Just like Mr. Grant Money had persevered while zooming around the Indy 500 track, young people should persist in their scholarship and grant applications, learning from rejections and continuously improving.

With his stylish charm and the wisdom of his high-speed adventure, Mr. Grant Money was ready to empower more young people with the tools they needed to secure grants and scholarships and speed toward their dreams.

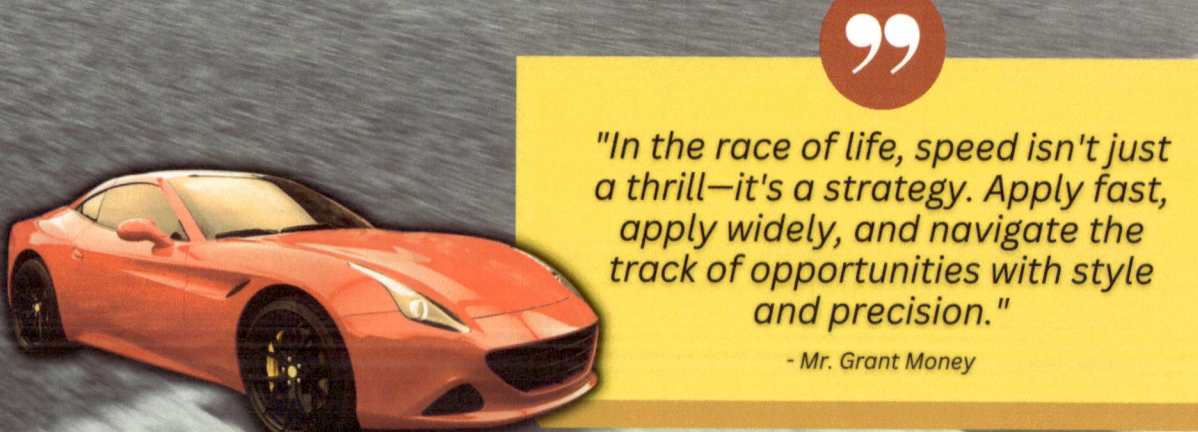

"In the race of life, speed isn't just a thrill—it's a strategy. Apply fast, apply widely, and navigate the track of opportunities with style and precision."

- Mr. Grant Money

Exercise: "Turbocharge Your Scholarship Success Roadmap"

Embark on this Turbocharge Your Scholarship Success Roadmap exercise with the determination to accelerate your scholarship journey. Speed, customization, perseverance, and continuous improvement will be your keys to success on the fast track towards securing grants and scholarships.

Steps:

1. Start Your Engines:
- Kick off the exercise by setting a clear goal for securing scholarships. Define the number, type, and value of scholarships you aim to win. This step lays the foundation for a focused and purposeful journey.

2. Scholarship Sprint Planning:
  Research and identify a minimum of 10 diverse scholarship opportunities that align with your goals. Categorize them based on fields, interests, and eligibility criteria. This comprehensive list will serve as your roadmap for the exercise.

3. Customization Pit Stop:
- Choose three scholarships from your list and craft customized essays tailored to each application. Emphasize your unique experiences and how they align with the respective scholarship's mission and values. This step refines your ability to create compelling, personalized application materials.

4. Speed Application Marathon:
- Set aside dedicated time to apply promptly to the three selected scholarships. Complete the entire application process, from gathering documents to submission. This fast-paced approach reinforces the importance of applying promptly and efficiently.

5. Perseverance and Feedback Loop:
- Reflect on any past rejections or setbacks in your scholarship journey. Identify key lessons learned and create a plan for improvement. Seek feedback from mentors, teachers, or peers on your application materials. This step emphasizes the value of perseverance and continuous improvement.

6. Networking Acceleration:

- Connect with at least three professionals, mentors, or individuals who have successfully secured scholarships. Gather insights into their strategies and experiences. Building this network adds valuable perspectives to your scholarship-seeking journey.

7. Create Your Fast-Track Resource Hub:

- Develop an interactive online platform or use existing resources to compile scholarship directories, application tips, and guidance. Ensure it is easily accessible and user-friendly. This step aligns with Mr. Grant Money's approach to making the path to securing grant money as fast and efficient as a high-speed race.

8. Review and Refine:

- Periodically review your progress and refine your scholarship strategy based on feedback, learnings, and evolving goals. This ongoing process ensures that your scholarship roadmap remains dynamic and aligned with your aspirations.

"Dress your dreams in the sleek attire of determination, rev up the engine of ambition, and speed down the lanes of opportunity with the flair of a true scholar-roadster."

- Mr. Grant Money

Discussion Questions

1. Mr. Grant Money draws a parallel between the pace of life and driving on the fast track. How do you interpret this metaphor, and how can applying the concept of speed and diversity in opportunities impact one's personal and professional growth?

2. Diversity of applications is highlighted as a key takeaway. Share your thoughts on the significance of applying to a wide range of opportunities. How do you believe this approach can enhance the chances of success, and have you personally experienced the benefits of diverse applications?

3. Customizing essays and documents is emphasized in the story. How important do you think personalization is in scholarship applications, and how can tailoring your materials enhance your chances of standing out among other applicants?

4. The story emphasizes both speed in applying promptly and perseverance in the face of challenges. How do you balance the need for swift action with the patience required to persevere through rejections and setbacks? Share your strategies for maintaining this delicate equilibrium.

5. Mr. Grant Money creates an online platform to share practical insights. In today's digital age, how do you envision the role of technology in empowering individuals in their educational and career pursuits? What features or resources would you consider essential in an online platform dedicated to scholarship success?

 Big Idea "Speed Scholar Workshops"

Organize workshops or webinars focused on efficient scholarship application strategies. These sessions could provide hands-on training for tailoring application materials, creating a diverse portfolio of submissions, and utilizing technology for faster and more effective searches. The aim is to empower participants with practical skills to navigate the scholarship landscape with speed and precision.

🔍 Word Search

Embark on a thrilling word search adventure inspired by the high-speed escapades of the ever-stylish Mr. Grant Money. As he revved up the engine at the iconic Indy 500, his journey became a metaphor for life's fast track.

Discover 15 words hidden in this puzzle that capture the essence of his wisdom on diverse applications, customized essays, prompt action, and perseverance.

Now, here are the 15 words for the word search puzzle based on the story:

I	U	E	N	I	G	N	E	Y	D	N	I	L	E
N	E	N	Y	O	C	I	L	H	G	I	H	O	O
E	V	Z	L	O	T	R	L	A	E	E	E	P	E
C	R	E	P	O	D	A	I	P	Z	T	N	P	S
R	P	I	P	H	E	C	R	V	I	D	I	O	C
H	S	P	A	H	M	E	H	S	M	I	L	R	H
C	U	R	E	G	I	I	T	P	O	V	A	T	O
E	P	I	N	R	T	I	T	E	T	E	N	U	L
L	R	E	W	I	S	N	N	E	S	R	E	N	A
G	O	O	I	C	N	E	E	D	U	S	R	I	R
P	M	E	S	W	D	D	V	I	C	I	D	T	S
T	P	O	D	I	E	V	D	E	E	T	A	I	H
I	T	E	O	N	P	P	P	P	R	Y	A	E	I
I	D	R	M	I	M	G	L	N	T	E	E	S	P

SPEED
THRILL
APPLY
ADRENALINE
SCHOLARSHIP
RACE
DIVERSITY
PROMPT
PERSEVERE
WISDOM
INDY
CUSTOMIZE
OPPORTUNITIES
HIGH
ENGINE

"Life's grand auction offers unique prizes to those who dare to bid on diverse experiences. Just as Mr. Grant Money embraced the thrill of speed, seize the opportunities with a blend of passion, strategy, and your own distinct flair."

SUCCESS STORIES

"Isabella Santos: Sowing Seeds of Sustainability"

In the bustling city of Los Angeles, where dreams collide with the reality of urban living, Isabella Santos emerged as a beacon of hope for environmental enthusiasts. As a Hispanic student navigating the complexities of her surroundings, Isabella's journey to a scholarship at Harvard is a tale of passion, perseverance, and a commitment to sustainable change.

Isabella's love for nature was nurtured in the heart of a concrete jungle. Growing up, she witnessed the environmental challenges faced by her community. Undeterred, she took it upon herself to be a catalyst for change. Her journey began with small acts – organizing local clean-up initiatives and educating her peers about the importance of environmental stewardship.

Understanding the power of education, Isabella sought ways to intertwine her passion for the environment with her academic pursuits. In high school, she spearheaded a student-led project focused on creating community gardens in underserved neighborhoods. The initiative not only addressed food insecurity but also became a symbol of resilience and sustainability.

Isabella's commitment to making a difference extended to her academic endeavors. In pursuit of her goal, she engaged in environmental research, collaborating with local experts to explore innovative solutions for urban sustainability. Her efforts bore fruit when she presented her findings at regional science fairs, catching the attention of Harvard's scholarship committee.

Harvard recognized not only Isabella's academic excellence but also her hands-on approach to solving real-world problems. In her application, Isabella outlined her vision for a sustainable future and the role she aspired to play in it. The scholarship interview process allowed her to articulate her passion and demonstrate the tangible impact of her initiatives.

In a statement that encapsulates her journey, Isabella Santos remarked, "Harvard is not just a destination; it's an opportunity to amplify my voice for environmental justice. The scholarship is not just a recognition of my past efforts but a belief in the potential for positive change in the future."

Isabella's story serves as an inspiration for those seeking scholarships with an emphasis on social and environmental impact. Her journey highlights the importance of proactive community engagement, research, and a clear articulation of one's vision in the pursuit of scholarships that align with personal values and ambitions.

As Isabella ventures into the halls of Harvard, she carries with her not just a passion for sustainability but the hopes of a community eager to see the seeds she planted in Los Angeles blossom into a global movement for environmental change.

Beyond Boundaries: The Symphony of Mr. Grant Money's Guidance

Echoes Of Determination, Effort, Action, And Focus In The Scholarship Quest

Mr. Grant Money's stylish demeanor remained unwavering as he embarked on yet another adventure, this time to the breathtaking Himalayas. He was dressed impeccably in a sleek charcoal gray suit, a crisp white shirt, and a burgundy silk tie that added a touch of sophistication. The choice of attire was a testament to his commitment to always look his best, even in the most adventurous of settings.

As he boarded the plane, his attire spoke volumes about his readiness for the new journey. The perfectly tailored suit and tie highlighted his preparedness, even as he ventured into the majestic Himalayan landscapes.

While onboard the plane, Mr. Grant Money took a moment to review some important letters. Among them was a heartfelt message from a young person in Nashville, Tennessee, requesting his help in securing scholarships. This letter was just one of 25 others that his trusted assistant, Joerje, had forwarded to him. Each letter represented a unique story, filled with dreams and aspirations.

Mr. Grant Money wanted to help each of these students, but the reality was that his schedule was packed, his private consultation fees were high, and the students were spread out across the nation. It was a challenge to provide individual assistance to everyone who reached out to him.

As he contemplated the predicament, an idea began to form. He realized that he could leverage his knowledge and expertise in a more affordable and cost-effective manner. Instead of one-on-one consultations, he decided to create a YouTube Channel dedicated to sharing tips, insights, and advice on securing grants and scholarships.

The YouTube Channel would serve as a platform where he could reach a broader audience, helping many students simultaneously. It was a way to make his expertise accessible to those who needed it most, regardless of their location or financial means.

Fast forward to a student in Kansas named Emily. She was diligent and determined, watching Mr. Grant Money's videos and applying the principles he shared. She was a shining example of how commitment and action could lead to success. With Mr. Grant Money's guidance, she navigated the scholarship application process with skill and determination.

Emily didn't just hope for scholarships to appear in her lap; she actively pursued them. She followed the advice from Mr. Grant Money's YouTube Channel, customizing her applications, applying to diverse scholarships, and applying promptly. Her diligence and focus paid off, and she secured several scholarships that eased the financial burden of her education.

Mr. Grant Money made a notion in his Golden Journal, noting down a powerful quote inspired by Emily's journey: "Where there is a will, there is a way." Just as students who want grants must make their own way, they must take determined action, focus, and effort. They need to be D.E.A.F. in a positive way, just as Emily had been: Determined, Effortful, Action-oriented, and Focused.

Emily's success and the impact of Mr. Grant Money's YouTube Channel became a source of inspiration for many students across the nation. It was a reminder that dreams were within reach when they were pursued with determination and the right guidance.

Exercise: "Grant Money Scholarship Success Blueprint."

Remember, just as Mr. Grant Money and Emily have shown, where there is a will, there is a way. Stay determined, take consistent action, and believe in your ability to achieve your dreams. Good luck!

Steps:

1. Define Your Goals and Dreams:
- Take a moment to clearly define your academic and career goals. Write down your dreams and aspirations, creating a roadmap for your future.

2. Research and Identify Scholarships:
- Use online resources, scholarship databases, and Mr. Grant Money's YouTube Channel to identify a diverse range of scholarships that align with your goals. Consider factors such as eligibility criteria, application requirements, and deadlines.

3. Customize Your Approach:
- Tailor your scholarship applications to showcase your unique strengths, experiences, and aspirations. Craft personalized essays and application materials that resonate with each scholarship's specific requirements.

4. Stay Proactive and Consistent:
- Regularly check for new scholarship opportunities and updates on Mr. Grant Money's YouTube Channel. Set aside dedicated time each week to work on scholarship applications and stay consistent in your efforts.

"In the grand tapestry of life, every thread of determination we weave contributes to the masterpiece of success. Each student holds the brush, and with every stroke of effort, they paint the portrait of their own brighter future."

- Mr. Grant Money

5. Build a Support Network:
- Connect with mentors, teachers, and peers who can provide guidance and support throughout the application process. Share your goals with them and seek feedback on your application materials.

6. Utilize Time Management Techniques:
- Develop a realistic schedule that allows you to balance your academic commitments, extracurricular activities, and scholarship applications. Use time management techniques to maximize productivity.

7. Take Action and Be Persistent:
- Actively apply for a variety of scholarships, even if the odds seem challenging. Embrace Mr. Grant Money's philosophy of being D.E.A.F.: Determined, Effortful, Action-oriented, and Focused. Be persistent in your pursuit of financial assistance.

8. Celebrate Your Achievements and Pay It Forward:
- Celebrate each successful scholarship application and share your journey with others. Consider creating your own platform or blog to inspire and guide fellow students. Paying it forward can create a positive ripple effect in the community.

"Just as a well-tailored suit enhances one's appearance, a well-tailored application enhances one's chances. Approach scholarship pursuits with the same precision in crafting your story, and you'll find that the seams of opportunity align perfectly in your favor."

- Mr. Grant Money

Discussion Questions

1. How does Mr. Grant Money's decision to create a YouTube Channel reflect a shift in the traditional ways of providing assistance, and what impact do you think this innovative approach has on reaching a wider audience of students seeking scholarships?

2. Considering the challenge Mr. Grant Money faced in providing individual assistance to all the students who reached out to him, do you think creating a YouTube Channel was the most effective solution? What other creative alternatives could he have explored to address this dilemma?

3. In Emily's case, the story emphasizes the importance of active pursuit and tailored efforts in securing scholarships. How can students strike a balance between following general advice, like that provided on Mr. Grant Money's YouTube Channel, and tailoring their strategies to their unique circumstances and goals?

4. Mr. Grant Money's quote, "Where there is a will, there is a way," became a guiding principle for him and Emily. In what ways do you think this mindset can be applied to pursuits beyond scholarships and education? Can determination and focused effort lead to success in various aspects of life?

5. Considering the increasing importance of online platforms for learning and mentorship, do you believe that initiatives like Mr. Grant Money's YouTube Channel represent a positive trend in making expertise and guidance more accessible? Are there any potential drawbacks or challenges associated with relying on such platforms for crucial information and advice?

 ## Big Idea "Scholarship Fair"

Organize a scholarship fair that brings together scholarship providers, educational institutions, and students under one roof. This physical event could provide a unique opportunity for students to meet face-to-face with potential scholarship sponsors and learn about various opportunities. Workshops and seminars conducted by scholarship experts, including Mr. Grant Money, could also be featured. The fair would not only facilitate direct connections but also create a supportive and motivating environment for students to pursue their educational dreams.

🔍 Word Search

Embark on an exciting word search adventure inspired by the remarkable journey of Mr. Grant Money to the enchanting Himalayas. As he navigates the landscapes in his impeccable charcoal gray suit, crisp white shirt, and burgundy silk tie, he discovers a new way to make education dreams come true for students across the nation.

In this puzzle, you'll find 15 words that capture the essence of Mr. Grant Money's transformative experience. The words are hidden in all directions—horizontally, vertically, diagonally, and even backward. So, sharpen your skills, and let the word search begin!

Now, here are the 15 words for the word search puzzle based on the story:

Y	M	H	I	M	A	L	A	Y	A	S	E	R	G
N	E	R	E	S	Y	T	A	D	E	A	F	N	R
O	R	O	M	I	M	E	N	O	O	Y	O	L	J
I	U	I	O	E	I	M	H	R	D	I	L	O	F
T	T	A	N	R	E	E	A	I	T	I	U	L	O
C	N	U	E	M	R	U	L	A	O	R	R	A	C
A	E	C	Y	I	A	I	N	O	N	T	L	A	U
G	V	N	T	I	G	I	A	A	E	T	D	U	S
R	D	T	I	E	M	Y	L	I	M	E	I	R	T
A	A	I	N	R	T	I	A	H	S	H	T	C	L
N	I	T	E	T	C	E	E	B	U	I	O	N	G
T	M	T	O	Y	O	U	T	U	B	E	G	R	N
M	E	S	P	I	H	S	R	A	L	O	H	C	S
D	V	S	I	A	E	C	N	A	D	I	U	G	C

GUIDANCE
ATTIRE
HIMALAYAS
FOCUS
JOURNAL
GRANT
YOUTUBE
DETERMINATION
MONEY
DILIGENT
DEAF
EMILY
SCHOLARSHIPS
ACTION
ADVENTURE

"Dreams don't come gift-wrapped; they require the wrapping of determination, tied with the ribbon of effort. The journey to success is a self-assembled package, where your actions and focus shape the destination. Remember, it's not about waiting for the stars to align; it's about aligning yourself with the stars."

SUCCESS STORIES

"Raj Gupta: Defying Doubts and Mastering the Financial Game"

In the suburban landscape of Edison, New Jersey, Raj Gupta's journey to a scholarship at the prestigious Wharton School of Business is a testament to the power of resilience, financial acumen, and a strategic game-plan. Born into a second-generation Indian-American family, Raj faced not only the typical challenges of adolescence but also the weight of societal expectations.

From an early age, Raj exhibited an innate knack for numbers and a passion for understanding the intricate dance of the stock market. However, as he ventured into his high school years, the corridors echoed with whispers of doubt. Classmates dismissed his financial aspirations as mere fantasies, and naysayers questioned the feasibility of a teenager from a modest background aiming for a finance powerhouse like Wharton.

Raj decided to transform negativity into motivation. Rather than succumb to the doubt, he channeled it into a meticulous scholarship game-plan. Recognizing that financial achievements are often built on a foundation of education, he sought out every opportunity to enhance his knowledge.

His journey involved countless late nights spent devouring financial literature, participating in online investment competitions, and seeking mentorship from professionals in the field. Raj's bedroom became a hub of financial analysis, adorned with stock charts, investment journals, and a determination that drowned out the noise of skepticism.

In the face of disparagement, Raj maintained a stoic focus on his goal. Instead of shying away from challenges, he embraced them, using setbacks as stepping stones to improvement. When classmates scoffed at his aspirations, he responded with academic excellence, earning top marks in advanced math and economics courses.

The turning point came when Raj participated in a national stock market simulation. His strategic acumen not only propelled him to victory but also caught the attention of scholarship committees. His scholarship application was a meticulous document outlining not just his academic achievements but also his ability to navigate the financial world with insight beyond his years.

In a statement that echoed both gratitude and determination, Raj Gupta expressed, "Every doubter, every negative word – they fueled my determination to prove that dreams backed by hard work are unstoppable. Wharton isn't just a destination; it's the platform from which I will redefine what's possible in the world of finance."

Raj's story resonates not just as a triumph over financial challenges but as an anthem for those who face skepticism in their pursuits. His journey illustrates that a well-crafted game-plan, a resilient spirit, and an unwavering commitment to one's aspirations can turn doubts into stepping stones towards success.

As Raj steps onto the campus of Wharton, he carries not just a passion for finance but a roadmap for others who dare to dream beyond the limitations imposed by circumstance. His story is a reminder that sometimes the most potent motivation arises from the doubters who unwittingly propel us toward our greatest achievements.

Scholarly Soiree: Mr. Grant Money's High-Flying Scholarly Sojourn

Soaring Above Hawaii, A Heartfelt Journey Through Scholarships, Sumptuous Meals, And The Transformative Power Of Encouragement.

Up, up and away they went as Mr. Grant Money found himself in a helicopter, soaring above the picturesque Hawaiian landscape. From high above, he gazed down upon various volcanoes, each a testament to the Earth's raw power and beauty. The sights that unfolded beneath him were nothing short of spectacular and left him in awe.

After a smooth landing, Mr. Grant Money and his colleague made their way to a fancy upscale restaurant. It was a place known for its exquisite cuisine and elegant ambiance, where they could indulge in a sumptuous meal while enjoying a delightful conversation.

As they savored their dishes, Mr. Grant Money's colleague, Scott Daniels, couldn't help but express his curiosity. He leaned forward and asked, "Mr. Grant Money, what drives you to be so committed to helping young people secure scholarships and do their best?"

Mr. Grant Money paused for a moment, reflecting on the question. He took a sip of his wine before answering. "It has a lot to do with my own experiences," he began. "I was fortunate to receive several scholarships myself, and this is my way of paying it forward. But there's one scholarship in particular that profoundly shaped my life."

With a sense of nostalgia, Mr. Grant Money continued, "It was a $1,500 scholarship that I received because of my art teacher, Mrs. Hudson, from Hillcrest High School. She saw something in me and recommended me for this scholarship. It changed the course of my future."

He elaborated, "This scholarship led to a two-week student apprenticeship experience on a university campus. It was during that time that I realized my potential and gained greater confidence. Surprisingly, I received three awards during that experience, the most of anyone. It was amazing for the young me. The mentoring, encouragement, and support I received during that time helped shape me into who I am today."

Mr. Grant Money's eyes sparkled with gratitude as he spoke. "That's why I encourage young people to give their best, always," he emphasized. "You never know who is watching you and what key they may have that can unlock a treasure that can benefit you for life."

With a sense of appreciation, Mr. Grant Money opened his Golden Journal, taking a few moments to write a short thank-you letter to Mrs. Hudson. In his letter, he expressed his heartfelt gratitude for the simple act that had changed his life. The scholarship he received, and the support and mentorship that came with it, had a rippling effect that continued to touch lives, even as the words were written.

As Mr. Grant Money closed his journal, he carried with him the profound belief that sometimes, a single act of encouragement and support can set a young person on a path toward greatness. He was committed to being the one who encouraged and supported the next generation of scholarship winners, just as he had been.

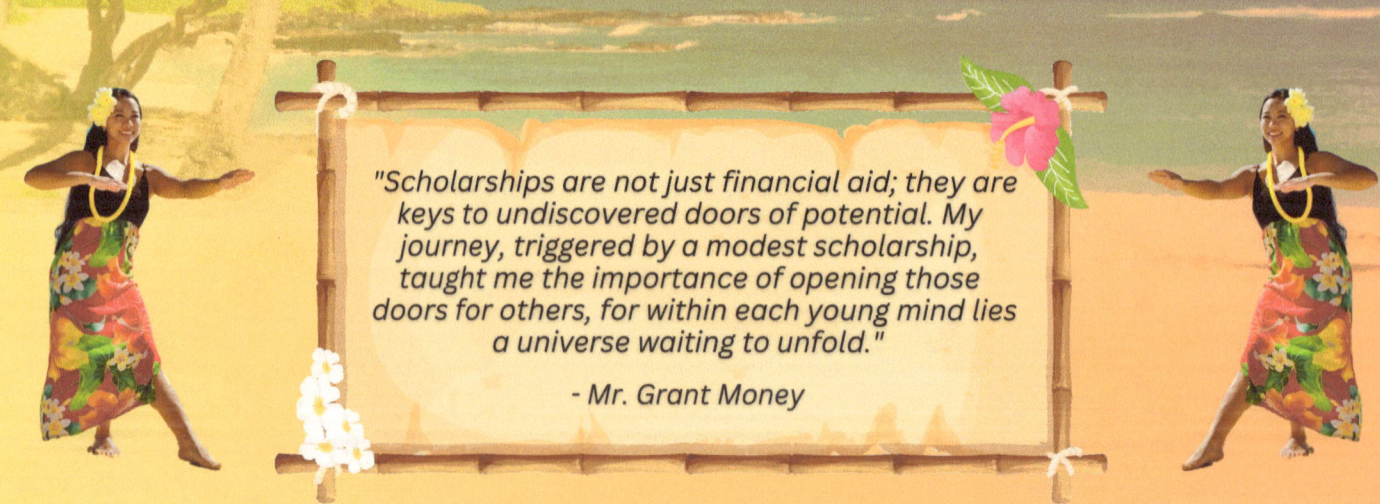

"Scholarships are not just financial aid; they are keys to undiscovered doors of potential. My journey, triggered by a modest scholarship, taught me the importance of opening those doors for others, for within each young mind lies a universe waiting to unfold."

- Mr. Grant Money

Exercise: "Unlock Your Potential"

Remember, the goal of this exercise is not only personal development but also contributing to a positive and supportive community. By unlocking your own potential, you can inspire and uplift those around you, creating a ripple effect of encouragement and success.

Steps:

1. Self-Reflection:
- Take some quiet time to reflect on your own experiences and identify a moment when someone's encouragement or support made a significant impact on your life. This could be a teacher, a friend, a family member, or anyone who played a role in shaping your journey.

2. Gratitude Journal:
- Create a gratitude journal or use your existing one. Write a heartfelt thank-you letter to the person you identified in step 1. Express your gratitude for their support and how it influenced your life positively. Be specific about the actions or words that had a lasting impact.

3. Identify Your Passion:
- Consider your interests and passions. What activities or subjects make you feel enthusiastic and alive? Write down at least three things that you are genuinely passionate about and would love to explore further.

4. Research Opportunities:
- Use online resources to research scholarships, mentorship programs, or apprenticeship opportunities related to your passions. Look for organizations or individuals offering support in those areas. Take note of the application processes and deadlines.

5. Reach Out for Guidance:
- Identify a mentor or someone knowledgeable in one of your passion areas. Reach out to them through email or social media, expressing your interest and seeking advice on how to pursue related opportunities. Don't be afraid to ask for guidance; people often appreciate enthusiasm and are willing to help.

6. Develop a Personal Development Plan:
- Based on your reflections and research, create a personal development plan. Outline short-term and long-term goals related to your passions. Break down these goals into actionable steps, making them realistic and achievable.

7. Community Involvement:
- Get involved in a community or group related to your interests. Attend events, workshops, or online forums where you can connect with like-minded individuals. Share your goals and learn from others who have similar aspirations.

8. Pay It Forward:
- As you progress on your journey, be on the lookout for opportunities to support and encourage others. Whether it's sharing insights, offering mentorship, or recommending someone for an opportunity, commit to being a positive force in someone else's life, just as Mr. Grant Money experienced.

"Life's true beauty lies not just in the awe-inspiring landscapes beneath a helicopter but in the transformative power of mentorship and encouragement. A single act of support can be the wind beneath the wings of a young dreamer, propelling them to soar to heights unimaginable."

- Mr. Grant Money

Discussion Questions

1. How do you think Mr. Grant Money's personal experience with receiving a scholarship shaped his commitment to helping young people secure scholarships, and why do you think he emphasizes the importance of paying it forward?

2. In the story, Mrs. Hudson played a crucial role in Mr. Grant Money's journey by recommending him for a scholarship. How can teachers and mentors impact the lives of their students beyond the classroom, and what role do you think educators play in shaping future opportunities for their students?

3. Mr. Grant Money mentions the $1,500 scholarship he received that had a profound impact on his life. How might financial support, even in seemingly modest amounts, contribute to significant transformations in a person's life, and what broader implications does this have for the importance of scholarships?

4. The story highlights the idea that a single act of encouragement and support can have a lasting impact on a young person's life. Can you think of any personal experiences or examples where a small gesture or piece of advice influenced your own or someone else's life in a meaningful way?

5. Mr. Grant Money emphasizes the idea that young people should always give their best because they never know who might be watching. How can cultivating a mindset of consistently giving one's best contribute to personal growth and open doors to unexpected opportunities, and have you personally witnessed or experienced the positive outcomes of such an approach?

 Big Idea "Establish a Scholarship Catalyst Program"

Create a program that identifies outstanding educators, like Mrs. Hudson, who have a keen eye for recognizing the potential in their students. The program could provide training and resources for teachers to actively seek out scholarship opportunities for their students, effectively becoming catalysts for transforming young lives. By institutionalizing and recognizing educators' efforts in steering students toward scholarships, this initiative would amplify the impact of individual acts of encouragement within the education system.

🔍 Word Search

Embark on a word-seeking adventure inspired by the remarkable journey of Mr. Grant Money, a philanthropist with a passion for uplifting young minds through scholarships. As you navigate this word search, immerse yourself in the vivid scenes of Mr. Grant Money's helicopter ride over the enchanting Hawaiian landscape and the sumptuous dining experience that followed.

Discover the words that encapsulate the essence of his commitment to empowering the next generation. Are you ready to uncover the hidden treasures within these letters?

Now, here are the 14 words for the word search puzzle based on the story:

```
T S I P O R H T N A L I H P
T G E E D U T I T A R G M P
M E N T O R I N G N L M L I
E N C O U R A G E M E N T H
L A S N P P E E R L E O L S
A T P E E O W P R S S S A R
N E T W L A T S T U A T N A
D S C P U E I E M N H A R L
S T C P E U G P N W H L U O
C A S A U S T A T T G G O H
A M E P T U E U N R I I J C
P E U I O A L E S T H A R S
E N N U L H E I J R G U L H
E T S C U R I O S I T Y R A
```

ENCOURAGEMENT
NOSTALGIA
SUMPTUOUS
GRATITUDE
PHILANTHROPIST
MENTORING
POTENTIAL
SCHOLARSHIP
AWE
JOURNAL
TESTAMENT
CURIOSITY
LANDSCAPE
ELEGANT

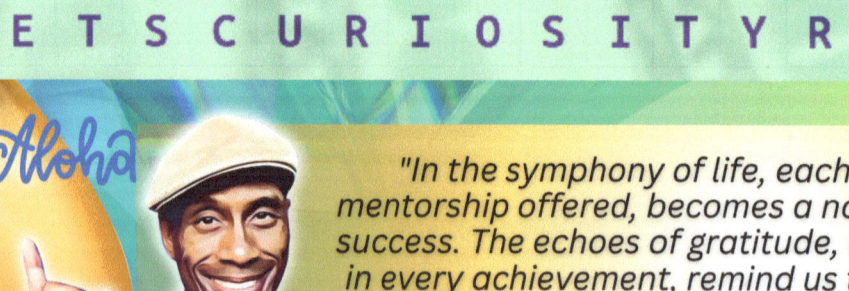

Aloha

"In the symphony of life, each scholarship awarded, every mentorship offered, becomes a note contributing to the melody o[f] success. The echoes of gratitude, written in golden journals and fe[lt] in every achievement, remind us that our actions today compose the soundtrack for someone else's tomorrow."

- Mr. Grant Money

SUCCESS STORIES

"Mia Chen: Striking the Right Chord Between Passion and Expectations"

In the eclectic city of San Francisco, where innovation dances with tradition, Mia Chen's journey to securing a scholarship at the prestigious Juilliard School of Music is a symphony of resilience, familial expectations, and the pursuit of her true passion. Born into a Chinese-American family deeply rooted in the sciences, Mia's desire to major in Fine Arts became a source of tension in her household.

The familiar narrative of immigrant families placing a premium on STEM careers weighed heavily on Mia's shoulders. The echoes of familial expectations whispered doubts in her ears, urging her to abandon her dreams of becoming a concert pianist. However, Mia was determined to find a harmonious balance between honoring her family's aspirations and staying true to her own.

Despite facing pressure to pursue a more conventional path, Mia continued to immerse herself in the world of music. Late nights were spent at the piano, translating her emotions into melodies that spoke louder than the dissenting voices around her. Instead of succumbing to familial expectations, Mia harnessed the dissonance as motivation to perfect her craft.

In her pursuit of a scholarship, Mia cast a wide net, applying to numerous programs that celebrated artistic excellence. She meticulously curated a portfolio that showcased not only her technical prowess but also the emotional depth she infused into her performances. Each application was a testament to her commitment to music as not just a career choice but a way of life.

The turning point came when Mia's impassioned rendition of a classical piece earned her a spot in a national music competition. The accolades that followed not only validated her talent but also caught the attention of scholarship committees. Mia's application process wasn't just a series of essays and interviews; it was an opportunity to articulate her journey of navigating familial expectations while pursuing her true calling.

In a poignant statement reflecting her journey, Mia Chen shared, "Juilliard is not just a stage; it's a canvas where I can paint my emotions through music. The scholarship isn't just financial aid; it's a validation that passion, when pursued with conviction, can resonate louder than any external expectations."

Mia's story resonates beyond the realm of music, serving as an anthem for those who grapple with the tug-of-war between familial expectations and personal aspirations. Her journey is a testament to the transformative power of art and the resilience required to forge a path that aligns with one's true passion.

As Mia prepares to enter the hallowed halls of Juilliard, she carries not just the weight of her family's expectations but also the melody of her own dreams. Her story is a reminder that sometimes, the most profound compositions emerge when we strike the right chord between honoring the past and composing our own future.

Dreams, Scepters, and Scholarship Super Bowls

From A Celestial Encounter To The Halls Of Greatness, The Dream That Sparked A Scholarship Super Bowl Revolution!

As the credits rolled on the movie screen, Mr. Grant Money found himself drifting into a bizarre dream world. A luminous figure named Jerla appeared, her extraterrestrial presence filling the dream space. With a touch on his forehead, visions of helping students on a global scale unfolded before him. Jerla then touched his golden scepter, causing it to gleam with an otherworldly glow.

Suddenly, Mr. Grant Money found himself squeezing the scepter, and the dream seamlessly transitioned into a real-life scenario. He was in Dallas, Texas, standing in the illustrious halls of Booker T. Washington High School for the Performing and Visual Arts. Though he felt invisible, his vision was crystal clear.

In the corridors of the school, he saw the echoes of greatness – seven towering figures who had once walked these very halls and emerged as exceptional talents:

⚜ **Erykah Badu**   ⚜ **Edie Brickell**   ⚜ **Yvonne Craig**   ⚜ **Owen Wilson**
⚜ **Norah Jones**   ⚜ **Keith Loftis**   ⚜ **Roy Hargrove**

As Mr. Grant Money observed, he realized that the dream had a purpose. It was more than just a surreal experience; it was a calling to make a real impact. Moving through the school, he encountered a group of students immersed in scholarship pursuits.

Inspired by the dream, Mr. Grant Money suggested an innovative idea that seemed to materialize in their minds: the concept of a "Scholarship Super Bowl." The idea was to create a competitive yet collaborative platform where students from different schools could compete over time to enhance their scholarship knowledge and vie for coveted prizes. The dream provided vivid details on how this Scholarship Super Bowl would work, fostering a spirit of healthy competition and learning.

Concept of the Scholarship Super Bowl

1. Teams and Challenges: Students form teams and take part in scholarship-themed challenges that test their research, writing, and presentation skills.

2. Point System: Each successful completion of a challenge earns points for the team. The challenges cover various aspects of scholarship applications, interviews, and portfolio development.

3. Mentorship Moments: Along the way, students receive mentorship from professionals, including Mr. Grant Money himself, guiding them through the intricacies of scholarship preparation.

4. Grand Celebration: The Super Bowl concludes with a grand celebration where the winning team is announced, and all participants are recognized for their efforts. Prizes include scholarship funds, mentorship opportunities, and resources for future endeavors.

As the dream unfolded the details of this concept, Mr. Grant Money felt a surge of excitement and motivation. The dream concluded with laughter, cheers, and a sense of accomplishment.

Suddenly, he awoke, wondering if it was all just a figment of his imagination. The golden scepter lay on his nightstand, its surface gleaming mysteriously. Was it a dream or a cosmic intervention? Mr. Grant Money pondered the possibilities, eager to embark on the next adventure that awaited him. The Scholarship Super Bowl concept lingered in his mind, a seed planted in the fertile soil of his philanthropic spirit, ready to blossom into reality.

Exercise: "Bringing the Scholarship Super Bowl to Life"

Objective: Develop the Scholarship Super Bowl concept into a tangible and impactful event that supports students in their pursuit of scholarships and educational opportunities.

Steps:

1. Research and Understand:
- Begin by researching existing scholarship competitions and educational challenges. Understand their formats, success stories, and potential areas of improvement.

2. Engage Stakeholders:
- Identify key stakeholders, including educators, students, professionals, and potential sponsors. Reach out to them to gauge interest and gather insights into what would make the Scholarship Super Bowl successful.

3. Formulate Rules and Challenges:
- Based on your research and stakeholder input, develop a comprehensive set of rules and challenges for the Scholarship Super Bowl. Ensure that the challenges cover a range of scholarship-related skills and knowledge areas.

4. Create a Point System:
- Establish a fair and transparent point system that rewards teams for their achievements in each challenge. Consider incorporating feedback from educators and professionals to make it comprehensive and reflective of real-world scholarship criteria.

"In the grand theater of dreams, where luminous visions meet the golden glow of opportunity, I've learned that the magic isn't in the spectacle but in the impact we make. The Scholarship Super Bowl isn't just a game; it's a transformative journey where students turn scholarship challenges into stepping stones to greatness."

- Mr. Grant Money

5. Secure Mentors and Judges:
- Reach out to professionals, including Mr. Grant Money, who can serve as mentors and judges for the competition. Ensure they are willing to offer mentorship moments and provide valuable feedback to participating students.

6. Plan the Grand Celebration:
- Envision and plan the grand celebration that marks the conclusion of the Scholarship Super Bowl. Consider logistics, venue, and ways to make it a memorable experience for participants. Explore potential partnerships for prizes and recognition.

7. Promote and Recruit:
- Develop a strategic promotional plan to recruit teams from different schools. Utilize social media, educational networks, and partnerships with schools to spread awareness about the Scholarship Super Bowl. Highlight the benefits and unique features of the competition.

8. Launch and Iterate:
- Launch the first edition of the Scholarship Super Bowl, closely monitoring its progress and gathering feedback from participants, mentors, and judges. Use this information to iterate and improve the competition for future editions.

9. Document and Share Success Stories:
- Throughout the Scholarship Super Bowl, document success stories, challenges overcome, and the impact on participating students. Share these stories through various channels to inspire others and attract more support for future iterations.

By following these steps, you can transform the dream-inspired concept of the Scholarship Super Bowl into a reality that empowers students on a global scale, just as Mr. Grant Money envisioned in his dream.

"In the symphony of life, each scholarship awarded, every mentorship offered, becomes a note contributing to the melody of success. The echoes of gratitude, written in golden journals and felt in every achievement, remind us that our actions today compose the soundtrack for someone else's tomorrow."

- Mr. Grant Money

Discussion Questions

1. What role do you think dreams or surreal experiences can play in shaping a person's sense of purpose or calling? How might Mr. Grant Money's dream with Jerla have influenced his actions and decisions in the real world?

2. Reflecting on the illustrious alumni of Booker T. Washington High School for the Performing and Visual Arts, what impact do you believe exceptional talents can have on a community and the world at large? How might the presence of these accomplished individuals inspire current and future students?

3. The Scholarship Super Bowl concept blends competition with collaboration, challenging students in scholarship-themed tasks. In what ways do you think this unique approach could enhance the learning experience and prepare students for future academic and professional challenges?

4. The dream involves a mentorship component, with professionals guiding students through scholarship preparation. How crucial do you think mentorship is in the educational journey, and how might it positively influence the development of young talents?

5. Considering the potential impact of the Scholarship Super Bowl, do you think similar creative initiatives could be effective in addressing educational challenges on a broader scale? How might such initiatives encourage innovation and engagement in education?

 Big Idea "Nationwide Scholarship Super Bowl Tour"

Transform the Scholarship Super Bowl concept into a nationwide tour that travels to various high schools and educational institutions. Mr. Grant Money could partner with sponsors, educational foundations, and celebrities to organize events in different cities, bringing the scholarship challenges, mentorship sessions, and grand celebrations to a broader audience. This touring approach would not only make the Scholarship Super Bowl more inclusive but also allow students from diverse backgrounds to participate in person. The tour could culminate in a national championship event, garnering media attention and further promoting the importance of scholarship preparation.

🔍 Word Search

Embark on a journey into the dream realm of Mr. Grant Money, where the boundaries between imagination and reality blur. As the credits rolled on the movie screen, an extraordinary tale unfolded, transporting Mr. Grant Money into a surreal world guided by an extraterrestrial presence named Jerla.

In this dream, a vision of global impact emerged, focusing on the noble endeavor of supporting students. Join Mr. Grant Money as he navigates through the illustrious halls of Booker T. Washington High School for the Performing and Visual Arts in Dallas, Texas, discovering echoes of greatness and an innovative idea that would shape the future – the "Scholarship Super Bowl."

Now, here are the 15 words for the word search puzzle based on the story:

W	O	R	J	S	A	L	L	A	D	A	A	A	U
A	A	C	O	H	A	H	E	D	J	E	B	O	S
S	O	E	N	E	R	E	S	S	R	E	I	A	U
H	N	N	E	M	C	O	U	C	D	E	R	D	D
I	S	R	S	H	R	N	A	E	A	Y	A	L	M
N	W	H	I	G	G	H	N	P	T	B	Y	M	A
G	E	I	A	R	N	E	E	T	C	I	Y	A	R
T	S	A	L	R	B	E	I	E	E	S	E	L	C
O	H	B	J	S	G	O	M	R	O	I	N	D	B
N	A	S	H	B	O	R	O	O	H	S	O	N	A
R	K	Y	A	M	A	N	O	K	U	O	M	O	K
R	Y	O	R	N	I	A	C	V	E	A	E	P	V
T	R	R	O	W	N	R	R	A	E	R	S	R	E
O	E	R	N	O	N	L	L	G	R	A	N	T	E

JONES
SCEPTER
JERLA
ROY
WILSON
BOOKER
DALLAS
MONEY
WASHINGTON
ERYKAH
HARGROVE
GRANT
BADU
DREAM
NORAH

"In the realm where dreams weave seamlessly into reality, a visionary concept emerged from the depths of the night—a Scholarship Super Bowl. It's not just a competition; it's a tapestry of talent, a fusion of knowledge, and a celebration of the extraordinary potential within students. In the corridors of learning, dreams take flight, guided by the golden scepter of inspiration."

- Mr. Grant Money

SUCCESS STORIES

"A Crescendo of Dreams: Malik Johnson's Jazz Odyssey from the Bayou to Berklee"

Have you ever heard a melody so rich, so soulful, that it carries the heartbeat of an entire city within its notes? This is the story of Malik Johnson, a young African American with a saxophone in his hand and a dream echoing through the vibrant streets of New Orleans.

In the heart of Louisiana's rhythmic soul, New Orleans, Malik Johnson's journey unfolds like a jazz composition, each note revealing a layer of his passion for music. A question lingers in the humid air: Can a dream, fueled by raw talent and nurtured against the backdrop of historic streets, find its crescendo on the grand stage of Berklee College of Music?

Malik's odyssey began in the vibrant tapestry of New Orleans, a city where music is not just heard but felt, where the echo of saxophones weaves through the jazz-laden air. Raised in a community where the beats of life synchronize with the pulse of the Mississippi, Malik's connection to music was inevitable. But what set him apart was not just his appreciation for the art; it was his burning desire to contribute his own notes to the ever-evolving jazz narrative.

Malik's practical journey towards achieving his dreams was a symphony of dedication and discipline. The saxophone, once a mere instrument, became an extension of his soul. Late nights were spent in intimate conversation with the brass and reeds, as he honed his skills in the shadows of iconic jazz clubs. From the historic Preservation Hall to the dimly lit corners of Frenchmen Street, Malik's saxophone echoed through the very veins of the city that birthed jazz.

His passion caught the attention of local mentors and musicians who recognized the spark within him. Malik embraced every opportunity to learn, often attending jam sessions where the legends of jazz had once graced the stage. But it wasn't just about playing the notes; it was about understanding the stories woven into each improvisation, the history etched in every chord.

And then came the defining moment—an announcement reverberating through the Big Easy like a jubilant brass band. Malik Johnson, the young saxophonist with dreams as vast as the Mississippi, had been awarded a scholarship to Berklee College of Music. The news rippled through the community, a testament to the power of dreams nurtured in the cradle of jazz.

As Malik embarks on his journey to Berklee, he reflects on the path that led him from the bayou to the hallowed halls of a prestigious institution. In his own words, Malik shares, "New Orleans is the heartbeat of my music, and Berklee is the stage where my heartbeat meets the world. This journey is not just mine; it's a testament to the resilience of dreams in the face of adversity."

Malik's story is an anthem for aspiring musicians, a testament to the idea that from the humblest beginnings can arise the most soul-stirring melodies. As he steps onto the global stage, saxophone in hand, Malik carries with him the spirit of New Orleans—a city that birthed jazz and now, through him, sends its melodies echoing across the world. The odyssey continues, a crescendo of dreams that inspires every student to believe that their unique notes can resonate far beyond the streets where their journey began.

Emerald City Insights: Scholarships and STEM Dreams

Join The Adventure As Mr. Grant Money Ignites Seattle's Scholarship Scene With A Golden Idea

Dressed in a sharp ensemble comprising a sleek dark brown suit, Mr. Grant Money found himself in the bustling city of Seattle, Washington, his golden scepter in hand. The recent dream lingered in his thoughts, and he felt a newfound sense of purpose as he explored the vibrant culture and technology scene of the Pacific Northwest.

Seattle's iconic Space Needle stood tall against the backdrop of the city, and the innovative spirit of the region captivated Mr. Grant Money. In a twist of fate, he found himself invited as a guest speaker at a STEM event hosted at the prestigious Garfield High School. With a confident stride, he entered the school auditorium, ready to connect with students passionate about science, technology, engineering, and mathematics.

Addressing the students, Mr. Grant Money shared insights into the world of scholarships, emphasizing their potential to support STEM dreams and innovative projects. During the Q&A session, a student named Brenda eagerly raised her hand, seeking advice on crafting a standout scholarship essay.

Mr. Grant Money smiled and offered Brenda and her peers five key points for creating an impactful scholarship essay:

1. **Authenticity**: "Tell your story truthfully. Scholarship committees want to connect with the real you, your aspirations, and your journey."

2. **Passion for STEM**: "Highlight your passion for STEM fields. Showcase how your experiences and projects have fueled your desire to make a difference in these areas."

3. **Future Impact**: "Paint a vivid picture of the impact you envision making in the future. How will your STEM pursuits contribute to positive change in your community and beyond?"

4. **Overcoming Challenges**: "Share the challenges you've faced and conquered. Scholarship committees appreciate resilience and determination."

5. **Unique Perspective**: "Showcase what makes you unique. Your perspective, experiences, and ideas are valuable assets in the pursuit of scholarships."

As the dialogue continued, Mr. Grant Money sensed the enthusiasm in the room. The dream's revelation about the Scholarship Super Bowl concept echoed in his mind, sparking an idea.

In a spontaneous moment, he suggested to the school administrator the concept of the first annual "MGM Scholarship Essay Week." The event would encourage students to participate in essay writing, culminating in winners and prizes. Community representatives would judge the essays, adding a layer of authenticity and community involvement.

To kickstart the initiative, Mr. Grant Money pledged a $5,000 prize to be added to the pot for the winning student. The administrator, inspired by the idea, announced the upcoming Scholarship Essay Week, providing students with two weeks to craft their essays.

The room buzzed with excitement as students embraced the challenge, motivated by the prospect of scholarships and the chance to showcase their STEM aspirations. Mr. Grant Money, satisfied with the positive energy he had ignited, left Garfield High School, his golden scepter glinting in the Seattle sunlight, ready for the next adventure that awaited him.

Exercise: "Crafting Your Impactful Scholarship Essay"

Objective: Develop a compelling scholarship essay following the guidance provided by Mr. Grant Money, with a focus on authenticity, passion for STEM, future impact, overcoming challenges, and showcasing a unique perspective.

Steps:

1. Reflect on Your Journey (Authenticity):
- Take some time to reflect on your personal journey, aspirations, and experiences. Identify key moments that have shaped your interest in STEM fields and your unique perspective.

2. Identify Passionate STEM Experiences:
- List specific experiences, projects, or activities that showcase your passion for science, technology, engineering, or mathematics. Consider how these experiences have influenced your desire to make a difference in these areas.

3. Envision Your Future Impact (Future Impact):
- Imagine the positive changes you aspire to make in your community and beyond through your STEM pursuits. Paint a vivid picture of the impact you hope to achieve and the contributions you plan to make.

4. Explore and Share Challenges Faced:
- Reflect on challenges you've faced on your journey. Identify obstacles you've overcome, demonstrating resilience and determination. These challenges could be academic, personal, or related to your STEM pursuits.

"In the grand symphony of scholarships, your essay is the solo that resonates with the hearts of those holding the golden scepter. Play it with authenticity, passion, and a melody that echoes your unique STEM journey."

- Mr. Grant Money

5. Highlight Your Unique Perspective:

- Consider what makes you unique – your background, experiences, and ideas. Explore how your perspective adds value to the field of STEM and distinguishes you from other applicants.

6. Outline Your Essay:

- Create a detailed outline for your scholarship essay. Organize your thoughts and experiences into a coherent structure, ensuring each key point (authenticity, passion, impact, challenges, uniqueness) is addressed.

7. Write the First Draft:

- Use your outline to write the first draft of your scholarship essay. Focus on expressing yourself authentically and passionately, incorporating specific examples to support your points. Pay attention to clarity, coherence, and word choice.

8. Seek Feedback and Revise:

- Share your draft with peers, teachers, or mentors. Gather constructive feedback on both content and writing style. Revise your essay accordingly, ensuring it aligns with Mr. Grant Money's advice and effectively communicates your unique story and aspirations.

By following these steps, you'll not only craft a standout scholarship essay but also gain valuable insights into your own journey, strengths, and aspirations in the STEM field.

"In the realm of scholarships, the essay is your passport to the future. Craft it with the ink of your experiences, the paper of your aspirations, and let it be a beacon that guides you toward the golden opportunities awaiting you."

- Mr. Grant Money

Discussion Questions

1. What role do you think Mr. Grant Money's attire and the symbolism of the golden scepter play in the narrative? How might these elements contribute to the overall theme or message of the story?

2. Discuss the significance of the Space Needle and the city of Seattle as a backdrop for Mr. Grant Money's visit. How does the setting influence the story, and what impact might it have on the character's sense of purpose and inspiration?

3. In crafting a standout scholarship essay, Mr. Grant Money emphasizes the importance of authenticity. Why do you think authenticity is crucial in scholarship essays, and how might it resonate with scholarship committees and readers? Can you think of any real-life examples where authenticity made a difference in a scholarship application?

4. The concept of the "MGM Scholarship Essay Week" introduces a community-driven approach to supporting students. How might involving community representatives in judging the essays enhance the credibility and impact of the initiative? What potential benefits and challenges do you foresee in such an approach?

5. Mr. Grant Money's advice includes showcasing a unique perspective in scholarship essays. How can students effectively convey their uniqueness in a crowded field of applicants? Can you think of examples where a unique perspective played a crucial role in someone's success in obtaining a scholarship or achieving a personal goal?

 Big Idea "Innovation Grants for STEM Projects"

Develop an Innovation Grants program aimed at supporting hands-on STEM projects initiated by students. This program would provide financial assistance, resources, and mentorship to students with innovative ideas and projects in science, technology, engineering, and mathematics. The grants could be awarded on a competitive basis, with a panel of experts evaluating the potential impact, creativity, and feasibility of each project. The goal is to encourage students to turn their STEM passions into tangible projects that address real-world challenges, fostering a culture of innovation and entrepreneurship within the student community.

🔍 Word Search

Welcome to the "Mr. Grant Money Word Search Puzzle" inspired by the captivating journey of Mr. Grant Money in the vibrant city of Seattle, Washington. Dressed in a sharp ensemble, armed with a golden scepter, Mr. Grant Money embarked on an adventure that led him to the heart of STEM enthusiasm at Garfield High School.

As he shared insights on scholarships and encouraged students to embrace their unique voices, a brilliant idea emerged – the "MGM Scholarship Essay Week." In the spirit of this exciting initiative.

Now, here are the 14 words for the word search puzzle based on the story:

T	N	A	R	G	I	T	E	N	C	T	I	I	S
L	H	R	H	C	S	F	S	T	T	H	N	T	
Y	I	D	N	H	M	N	T	N	A	R	A	E	N
A	I	L	S	A	O	E	E	L	T	T	A	E	S
C	N	E	O	L	N	T	M	A	V	Y	S	A	S
O	N	I	N	L	E	M	O	N	R	A	A	D	C
M	O	F	A	E	Y	M	A	I	N	G	G	V	E
M	V	R	T	N	A	T	P	O	E	C	U	E	P
U	A	A	N	G	D	T	I	L	T	S	N	N	T
N	T	G	E	E	L	S	S	T	R	S	I	T	E
I	I	S	A	S	S	E	A	L	E	Y	Q	U	R
T	O	Q	V	A	S	E	R	E	E	S	U	R	S
Y	N	U	P	T	G	A	Q	N	T	T	E	E	D
S	C	H	O	O	L	N	Y	E	L	R	S	I	Y

ADVENTURE
PASSION
GARFIELD
ESSAY
GRANT
STEM
MONEY
SCHOOL
SEATTLE
COMMUNITY
SCEPTER
INNOVATION
CHALLENGE
UNIQUE

"Amidst the towering dreams and innovative ambitions, Garfield High School became more than a backdrop; it became the canvas on which students painted their visions of a brighter future. In the vibrant tapestry of Scholarship Essay Week, each word penned by the students was a brushstroke, creating a masterpiece of aspirations that would shape the landscape of tomorrow."

- Mr. Grant Money

SUCCESS STORIES

"Unleashing Innovation: Zara Ahmed's Silicon Symphony at MIT"

"In the realm of technology, innovation becomes a bridge to inclusion—a gateway to a world where everyone, regardless of ability, can thrive and contribute. My journey is not just about code; it's about building that bridge, one line at a time."*
— Zara Ahmed

Zara Ahmed, a tech trailblazer, sees innovation as a bridge to inclusion, a gateway for all to thrive in the realm of technology. In the dynamic heart of Silicon Valley, Zara's story unfolds—a testament to passion, perseverance, and an unwavering commitment to inclusivity. Her journey transcends the ordinary, driven by a purpose that goes beyond code, aiming to build a tapestry of accessibility and empowerment through technology.

From the outset, Zara's fascination with technology is purposeful, leading her into Computer Science with a focus on developing assistive technologies for those with disabilities.

Her story is a narrative of practical strides marked by tireless dedication, groundbreaking initiatives, and a deep immersion in the challenges faced by individuals with disabilities. Zara collaborates, engages in community dialogue, and seeks solutions beyond conventional technological boundaries, becoming a beacon of hope for the unheard voices in the tech landscape.

Zara's innovative contributions resonate through Silicon Valley, reaching the ears of the Massachusetts Institute of Technology (MIT). MIT, recognizing the transformative potential of her work, awards Zara a scholarship—an acknowledgment not only of her academic prowess but of her commitment to using technology for societal betterment.

As Zara prepares for her MIT journey, she reflects on the significance of her story, emphasizing the role of technology as a language that can either build walls or break barriers. Her mission is clear: to use code as a catalyst for change, creating a digital world where everyone is seen, heard, and included.

Zara Ahmed, the visionary coder advocating for inclusivity, extends an invitation to every student to recognize the transformative power of their passions. Her story isn't just personal success; it's a call to action for a generation of technologists to use their skills for the greater good. Stepping into MIT, Zara carries the dreams of a more accessible and inclusive future, where technology speaks volumes about empathy, innovation, and the limitless possibilities that lie ahead.

SCHOLARSHIP JAZZ IN NEW ORLEANS

Big Easy Rhythms: Scholarship Jazz in New Orleans

Unveiling Scholarly Secrets from The Vibrant Streets Of New Orleans

Dressed in a vibrant ensemble that captured the spirit of New Orleans, Mr. Grant Money, his sharp attire reflecting the lively colors of the city, strolled through the historic streets of the French Quarter. The sound of jazz permeated the air as he made his way to a vibrant gathering where a lively Second Line procession was about to begin.

With his golden scepter in hand, Mr. Grant Money joined the jubilant crowd, eager to experience the unique cultural phenomenon that is the Second Line. The brass band started playing, and the rhythm of drums, trumpets, and trombones filled the streets. The infectious energy of the Second Line took hold, and soon, Mr. Grant Money found himself dancing and twirling alongside the revelers.

As the parade made its way through the colorful streets, Mr. Grant Money marveled at the spirited celebration of life, community, and resilience that the Second Line embodied. Amidst the lively tunes, he couldn't help but notice the parallels between the vibrant rhythm of the Second Line and the journey of scholarship pursuit.

In a moment of inspiration, Mr. Grant Money addressed the crowd, drawing lessons from the lively Second Line:

1. Find Your Rhythm: "Just as in the Second Line, each of you has a unique rhythm in your scholarship journey. Find your groove, embrace your strengths, and let your passion guide you."

2. Celebrate Community: "The Second Line thrives on community spirit. Similarly, in your pursuit of scholarships, remember the power of collaboration and supporting one another. Lift each other up!"

3. Dance with Resilience: "Life, like the Second Line, is full of twists and turns. Dance through challenges with resilience. Every step you take brings you closer to your goals."

4. Embrace Diversity: "Look around. The Second Line welcomes all, celebrating diversity. In your scholarship journey, embrace the diversity of ideas, experiences, and backgrounds. It's what makes your story unique."

5. March to Your Own Beat: "In the Second Line, everyone dances to their own beat. Similarly, don't be afraid to march to your own rhythm in the pursuit of your dreams. Let your individuality shine."

As the lively Second Line continued, Mr. Grant Money, feeling the vibrant energy of New Orleans, made a mental note to capture these valuable lessons in his Golden Journal. The city's unique charm and the rhythm of the scholarship pursuit had intertwined in a lively dance, leaving everyone with a sense of celebration and inspiration.

"Just as in the Second Line, each of you has a unique rhythm in your scholarship journey. Find your groove, embrace your strengths, and let your passion guide you. Your scholarship pursuit is your personal melody, and when you dance to it, success will be your grand finale."

- Mr. Grant Money

Exercise: "Scholarship Strengths Assessment Tool"

Objectives: The Scholarship Strengths Assessment Tool is designed to help high school students identify and highlight their unique strengths and qualities, empowering them to craft compelling scholarship applications. By recognizing and showcasing individual strengths, students can enhance their scholarship prospects and stand out among applicants.

Steps:

1. Self-Reflection:
- Consider your academic achievements, extracurricular activities, and personal experiences.
- Reflect on challenges you've overcome and skills you've developed.

2. Identify Your Strengths:
- Rate yourself on a scale of 1 to 5 (1 being low, 5 being high) for each attribute.
- Be honest and consider feedback from teachers, mentors, or peers.

3. Academic Achievements:
- Analytical Skills.
- I excel in critical thinking, problem-solving, and data analysis.
- Subject Proficiency.
- I have a strong understanding of specific subjects or areas of study.
- Research Skills.
- I am skilled in conducting research and synthesizing information.

4. Extracurricular Activities:
- Leadership
- I have held leadership roles in clubs, sports, or community organizations.
- Teamwork
- I work effectively in team settings and collaborate well with others.
- Initiative
- I take the initiative to start new projects or contribute innovative ideas.

5. Personal Qualities:
- Resilience
- I bounce back from setbacks and challenges.
- Adaptability
- I can adapt to new situations and thrive in diverse environments.
- Creativity

6. Community Involvement:
- Volunteerism
- I actively participate in community service and volunteer initiatives.
- Social Impact.
- I am involved in projects that contribute positively to society.
- Civic Engagement.
- I am passionate about civic responsibilities and community betterment.

7. Communication Skills:
- Written Communication.
- I can articulate ideas effectively in writing.
- Verbal Communication.
- I am confident and articulate in verbal communication.
- Public Speaking.
- I can confidently speak in public or group settings.

8. Special Skills or Talents:
- Artistic Abilities.
- I have talents in music, visual arts, or performing arts.
- Technical Skills.
- I possess technical skills (coding, design, etc.) that set me apart.
- Language Proficiency.
- I am proficient in multiple languages.

Use the insights gained from this assessment to tailor your scholarship applications. Highlighting your unique strengths will make your application more compelling and increase your chances of securing scholarships that align with your individual qualities and aspirations.

"The Second Line thrives on community spirit. Similarly, in your pursuit of scholarships, remember the power of collaboration and supporting one another. Lift each other up! Together, we can create a scholarship symphony that echoes with the success of the entire community."

- Mr. Grant Money

Discussion Questions

1. Mr. Grant Money encourages individuals to find their unique rhythm in their scholarship journey. How can individuals identify and embrace their own academic rhythm, and what role does self-awareness play in navigating the twists and turns of scholarship pursuits?

2. In drawing a parallel between the Second Line's community spirit and scholarship, Mr. Grant Money emphasizes the importance of collaboration. How can a sense of community and support among scholarship seekers enhance the overall experience and increase success rates?

3. Mr. Grant Money draws a comparison between dancing through challenges in life and navigating scholarship pursuits with resilience. What are some practical strategies for maintaining resilience in the face of setbacks or obstacles in the pursuit of educational goals?

4. The Second Line celebrates diversity, and Mr. Grant Money encourages scholarship seekers to do the same. How does embracing diversity in ideas, experiences, and backgrounds contribute to a richer scholarship journey, and how can it positively impact one's educational and personal development?

5. Mr. Grant Money advises individuals to march to their own beat in the pursuit of their dreams. How can scholarship seekers strike a balance between conforming to traditional expectations and embracing their individuality, and what benefits might this bring to their academic and personal growth?

 Big Idea "Resilience Dance Workshops"

Organize workshops and events inspired by the concept of "Dance with Resilience." These workshops could combine elements of dance and motivational coaching to help students navigate challenges in their academic pursuits. By teaching resilience through movement and inspirational guidance, the Resilience Dance Workshops aim to equip scholarship seekers with the skills to overcome obstacles gracefully. The workshops could be conducted in educational institutions or as community events, bringing a unique and engaging approach to building resilience in the pursuit of academic goals.

🔍 Word Search

Embark on a spirited journey through the vibrant streets of the French Quarter with Mr. Grant Money! Dressed in a lively ensemble that mirrored the colors of New Orleans, he ventured through historic streets, captivated by the infectious rhythm of a Second Line celebration.

Join Mr. Grant Money in this word search puzzle inspired by the lively dance of the Second Line and the valuable lessons he shared with the jubilant crowd.

Now, here are the 15 words for the word search puzzle based on the story:

I	B	L	S	C	E	P	T	E	R	H	O	T	C
I	N	R	E	S	I	L	I	E	N	C	E	R	O
D	L	D	V	B	R	R	N	Y	S	A	C	E	L
I	R	L	I	E	C	S	N	T	I	M	E	V	L
V	Y	N	R	V	S	O	J	T	E	H	L	E	A
E	R	E	S	A	I	O	E	S	N	T	E	L	B
R	S	A	R	S	U	D	N	I	S	Y	B	E	O
S	E	B	S	R	R	I	U	I	C	H	R	R	R
I	A	A	N	D	I	H	B	A	O	R	A	S	A
T	P	E	N	O	B	I	R	E	L	A	T	H	T
Y	Y	N	G	O	L	D	E	N	C	I	E	N	I
L	E	U	O	T	P	T	B	A	N	D	T	D	O
S	C	H	O	L	A	R	S	H	I	P	C	Y	N
R	D	D	I	H	Y	T	I	N	U	M	M	O	C

Word list:

PASSION
BAND
INDIVIDUALITY
COLLABORATION
SCEPTER
SCHOLARSHIP
REVELERS
JOURNEY
DIVERSITY
BRASS
RESILIENCE
GOLDEN
RHYTHM
COMMUNITY
CELEBRATE

"Life, like the Second Line, is full of twists and turns. Dance through challenges with resilience. Every step you take brings you closer to your goals. The journey may have its unpredictable rhythms, but with resilience as your partner, you can waltz through obstacles and emerge victorious in your pursuit."

- Mr. Grant Money

SUCCESS STORIES

"Bridging Borders: Leila Khan's Journey from Queens to Georgetown"

It was a brisk autumn day in Queens, New York, when Leila Khan found herself standing at the crossroads of tradition and ambition. She recalls the vibrant tapestry of her Pakistani heritage interwoven with the urban rhythm of Queens, a borough that thrives on diversity. Little did she know that her story, much like the city around her, would become a mosaic of resilience, cultural exploration, and the pursuit of global harmony.

Leila's journey began as a young Pakistani American, navigating the delicate balance between her family's deeply rooted traditions and the boundless opportunities that America promised. As she walked the bustling streets of Queens, where the aroma of diverse cuisines wafted through the air, Leila felt the weight of cultural expectations and the tug of her own aspirations.

The turning point came during a family gathering, where discussions echoed with the resonance of two worlds colliding. Leila, inspired by the rich mosaic of cultures around her, shared her dream of studying International Relations—a path that seemed alien in the context of her traditional upbringing. The room fell silent, and for a moment, Leila felt the weight of cultural expectations threatening to eclipse her ambitions.

But it was in that silence that Leila found her voice—a voice that would go on to challenge stereotypes, foster understanding, and bridge the gaps between nations. Undeterred by the cultural barriers, she embarked on a journey of self-discovery and advocacy that would redefine her narrative.

Leila's practical steps towards her goal were a testament to her commitment to fostering cultural understanding. She actively engaged in community dialogues, organizing events that celebrated the rich tapestry of diversity in Queens. Her initiatives ranged from cultural exchange programs to workshops on diplomacy, aiming to break down stereotypes and build bridges of understanding.

The ripple effect of Leila's efforts reached beyond her community and into the corridors of academia. Georgetown University, impressed by her advocacy work and the tangible impact she was making, awarded Leila a scholarship to pursue her passion for International Relations. The news was not just a personal victory but a triumph for everyone who dared to challenge cultural norms in pursuit of their dreams.

Reflecting on her journey, Leila shares, "Queens is where my roots are, and Georgetown is where I learned to spread my wings. Every cultural barrier I faced became a stepping stone to understanding, and every conversation became a bridge to a more harmonious world."

As Leila steps onto the campus of Georgetown, she carries with her the stories of Queens—the borough that shaped her, challenged her, and ultimately propelled her towards success. Her narrative is not just a personal achievement but an invitation for every student to embrace their cultural identity while fearlessly pursuing their dreams. Leila Khan, a symbol of resilience and diplomacy, reminds us that the pursuit of education can be a powerful catalyst for change, transcending cultural boundaries and fostering a world where understanding triumphs over prejudice.

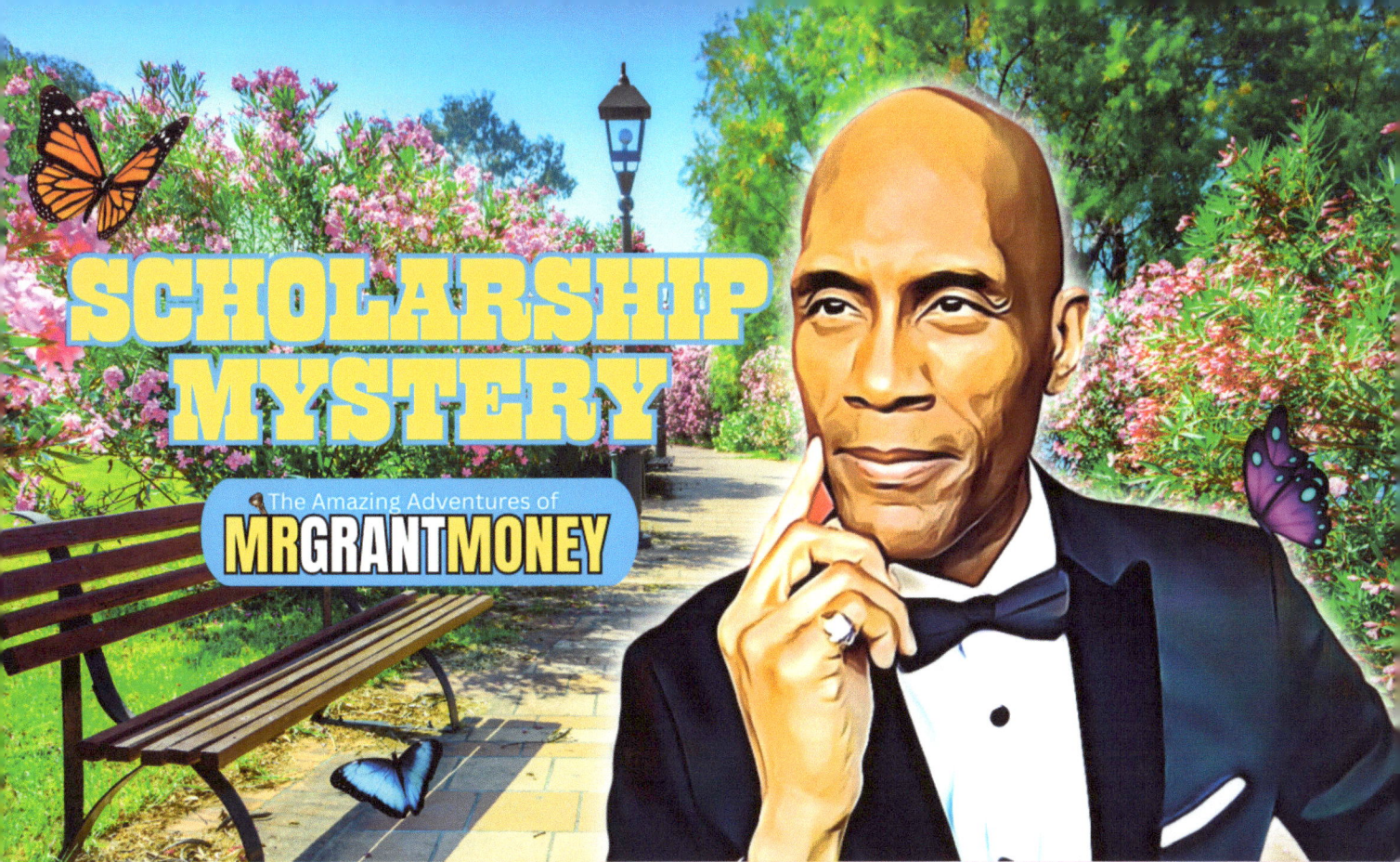

Beyond the Nap: A Butterfly's Gift of Collective Scholarship Mastery

*Join Mr. Grant Money's Quest To Transform
Individual Pursuits Into Shared Triumphs*

As Mr. Grant Money sat in the serene park, surrounded by nature's beauty, he felt a sense of calm wash over him. The vibrant colors of the flowers and the gentle rustle of leaves provided the perfect backdrop for a moment of reflection.

As he listened to soothing melodies through his earplugs, the tranquility of the park lulled him into a brief nap. During this short reprieve, a delicate butterfly landed gracefully on his shoulder. The butterfly seemed to exude an ethereal energy, and Mr. Grant Money felt a connection beyond the ordinary.

In a silent exchange of energy, Mr. Grant Money understood that the butterfly held a special message for him. It was as if Jerla, the cosmic being, had taken on this delicate form to impart more wisdom and ideas for helping students secure scholarships.

In the language of unspoken understanding, the butterfly conveyed additional insights to Mr. Grant Money, expanding upon the ideas he had already gathered. As he awoke, Mr. Grant Money felt invigorated with a renewed sense of purpose to share these collective strategies with students worldwide.

The next day, Mr. Grant Money took to his online platforms, sharing the butterfly-inspired insights with students eager to embark on their scholarship journeys. The ideas flowed like a cascade of possibilities, providing a roadmap for success in the pursuit of financial aid.

"Embrace the collective strength of shared knowledge," he urged, encouraging students to engage in scholarship brainstorming sessions. "Let each idea be a stepping stone towards a brighter future."

"Challenge yourselves monthly," he continued, "and turn the pursuit of scholarships into a shared journey. Celebrate each application submitted, knowing you're part of a community striving for success."

"Peer editing is not just about refining essays; it's about building a network of support," Mr. Grant Money emphasized. "Your fellow students are valuable allies on this quest, offering insights that can elevate your applications."

The butterfly's guidance echoed in his words as Mr. Grant Money encouraged students to participate in scholarship workshops and engage with professionals. "Gather like a flock of determined birds, absorbing the wisdom of those who have soared to great heights before you."

"Transform research into a collective adventure," he suggested, evoking the spirit of the butterfly's delicate flight. "Host research parties, explore scholarship databases together, and uncover opportunities that resonate with your dreams."

With each suggestion, Mr. Grant Money felt the butterfly's presence, a symbol of transformation and the boundless potential within each student. The scholarship journey wasn't just an individual pursuit; it was a collective endeavor, a symphony of efforts resonating through time and space.

As the butterfly fluttered away, leaving behind a trail of inspiration, Mr. Grant Money continued to share the wisdom received in the park. His online platforms became a hub of scholarship insights, each idea a testament to the collaboration between human and cosmic forces, guiding students on their unique paths toward success.

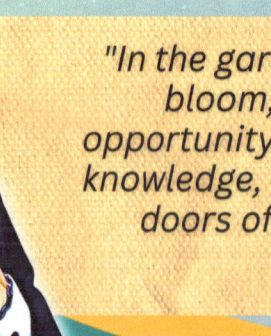

"In the garden of scholarships, each idea is a vibrant bloom, and together, we create a tapestry of opportunity. Embrace the collective strength of shared knowledge, for in unity, we find the key to unlocking the doors of financial aid and educational dreams."

- Mr. Grant Money

Exercise: "Butterfly Scholarship Quest"

Objective: Develop a collective and empowering approach to scholarship pursuit, drawing inspiration from the wisdom shared by the cosmic butterfly.

Steps:

1. Create a Scholarship Brainstorming Circle:
- Form a small group of like-minded students interested in pursuing scholarships. Schedule regular brainstorming sessions where each member contributes unique ideas and strategies. Emphasize the power of collective thinking and diversity of perspectives.

2. Monthly Challenge Commitment:
- Establish a monthly challenge for the group. Encourage each member to set a personal goal for scholarship applications, research, or skill development. Celebrate achievements at the end of each month, fostering a sense of shared progress.

3. Peer Editing Network Building:
- Initiate a peer editing system within the group. Exchange scholarship essays and application materials for constructive feedback. Emphasize the importance of building a supportive network for mutual growth and improvement.

4. Scholarship Workshops and Professional Engagement:
- Organize regular scholarship workshops within the group, inviting professionals or successful scholarship recipients to share their experiences. Encourage group members to attend webinars, conferences, or networking events related to scholarships.

5. Flock of Determined Birds - Mentorship Program:
- Establish a mentorship program within the group. Pair experienced scholarship seekers with newcomers, creating a supportive mentor-mentee dynamic. Facilitate knowledge exchange and guidance sessions.

6. Collective Adventure Research Parties:
- Host research parties where group members explore scholarship databases together. Share interesting findings, potential opportunities, and tips for effective research. Foster a collaborative and adventurous spirit in the pursuit of scholarship information.

7. Symbolic Butterfly Reflection Journals:
- Introduce individual reflection journals within the group. Encourage members to document personal growth, insights gained, and experiences throughout their scholarship journey. Reflect on the symbolic nature of the butterfly as a reminder of transformation and potential.

8. Online Platform for Collective Wisdom Sharing:
- Create a dedicated online platform (e.g., a shared document or forum) for the group to share insights, resources, and success stories. Develop a space where members can inspire and support each other, extending the collaborative effort beyond physical meetings.

Remember, the Butterfly Scholarship Quest is not just about individual success; it's about fostering a sense of community, shared learning, and collective empowerment on the scholarship journey.

> *"Let the pursuit of scholarships be a shared journey, a monthly challenge that transforms aspirations into achievements. Celebrate every submitted application as a triumph not just for yourself but as a part of a community striving for success. In the symphony of scholarship seekers, your notes harmonize with the collective melody of triumph."*
>
> - Mr. Grant Money

Discussion Questions

1. What role do you think nature and serenity play in fostering creativity and a sense of purpose, as illustrated in Mr. Grant Money's experience in the park? How might these elements positively influence one's approach to problem-solving, such as in the pursuit of scholarships?

2. In the story, the butterfly serves as a symbolic messenger, imparting additional insights to Mr. Grant Money. If you were to choose a symbolic messenger for your own journey, what form would it take, and what message or guidance do you imagine it might convey to you in your pursuit of personal or academic goals?

3. Mr. Grant Money emphasizes the importance of embracing the collective strength of shared knowledge. How have you personally benefited from collaborative efforts or group brainstorming sessions, especially when it comes to tackling challenges or pursuing opportunities? Share a specific experience that highlights the power of shared knowledge in your life.

4. The story suggests turning scholarship applications into a shared journey and celebrating each milestone as part of a community striving for success. How do you envision creating or being part of such a supportive community in your academic or professional pursuits? What benefits do you think come from sharing the journey with others?

5. The butterfly's guidance encourages students to engage in scholarship workshops, peer editing, and research parties. Reflect on your own approach to scholarship applications or any significant goals. How might incorporating these collective strategies enhance your preparation and increase your chances of success? Share specific steps you could take to implement these ideas into your own journey.

 Big Idea "Scholarship Adventure Kits"

Take the concept of transforming research into a collective adventure and create "Scholarship Adventure Kits." These kits could be physical or digital resources containing tools, guides, and interactive materials designed to make the scholarship application process more engaging and collaborative. The kits might include themed monthly challenges, prompts for scholarship brainstorming sessions, and resources for effective peer editing. By turning the scholarship journey into an exciting and shared experience, students can stay motivated and inspired throughout the application process, fostering a sense of community and purpose.

🔍 Word Search

Embark on a transformative journey with the Mr. Grant Money Wordsearch Puzzle, inspired by a unique encounter in a serene park. As Mr. Grant Money basked in the tranquility of nature, a cosmic messenger in the form of a delicate butterfly bestowed upon him invaluable insights for students seeking scholarships.

The puzzle features intricately woven into the fabric of this enchanting tale. Explore the depths of scholarship wisdom as you unravel the puzzle and embrace the collective strength of shared knowledge.

Now, here are the 14 words for the word search puzzle based on the story:

C	O	M	M	U	N	I	T	Y	O	N	E	C	E
I	U	O	S	E	E	M	O	N	E	Y	S	L	B
P	W	A	D	V	E	N	T	U	R	E	C	T	U
I	S	S	W	N	E	E	N	T	L	P	C	A	T
H	T	E	I	T	S	D	N	E	O	R	U	T	T
S	H	F	S	G	O	I	E	H	N	I	S	G	E
R	G	E	D	N	P	T	U	K	S	R	S	R	R
A	I	Y	O	S	R	I	C	R	E	R	E	A	F
L	S	K	M	R	U	N	I	O	V	T	C	N	L
O	N	R	S	C	P	G	N	W	D	E	C	T	Y
H	I	A	P	P	V	G	U	T	E	U	U	D	F
C	Y	P	C	E	I	E	F	E	P	I	S	N	R
S	D	P	C	S	U	M	S	N	P	L	H	T	I
Y	P	A	C	O	L	L	E	C	T	I	V	E	A

GRANT
MONEY
PARK
ADVENTURE
NETWORK
EDITING
PURPOSE
WISDOM
COMMUNITY
BUTTERFLY
SUCCESS
COLLECTIVE
INSIGHTS
SCHOLARSHIP

"Amidst the blooming flowers and fluttering butterflies, Mr. Grant Money uncovered the secret to success – a shared quest for knowledge and support. Like a delicate butterfly landing on his shoulder, inspiration alighted upon him.

- Mr. Grant Money

SUCCESS STORIES

"Igniting Change: Mateo Rodriguez's Expedition from Reservation to Harvard"

Igniting change from the heart of Albuquerque, New Mexico, Mateo Rodriguez stands as a beacon of resilience, dynamism, and unyielding passion. Born on a Native American reservation, Mateo's journey isn't just a pursuit of education; it's a mission to preserve and promote the very essence of his heritage—the indigenous languages that echo through the ancient landscapes of his people.

Mateo's odyssey began with a fervent determination to break the cycle of linguistic erosion that threatened to silence the rich narratives of his ancestors. Armed with a purpose that echoed across the mesas and canyons of his reservation, Mateo took on the formidable task of not only learning but revitalizing indigenous languages that had weathered centuries of change.

His journey was a symphony of action—a commitment that went beyond the confines of textbooks and classrooms. Mateo immersed himself in the daily lives of his community, engaging with elders, storytellers, and language keepers. His days were spent not just in the pursuit of academic excellence but in the trenches of cultural preservation, where the pulse of tradition thrived against the relentless march of time.

Mateo's practical approach to securing his scholarship to Harvard was a testament to his tireless efforts. He initiated language revitalization programs, organized community workshops, and collaborated with linguists and educators to develop innovative strategies for language preservation. His actions rippled through the reservation, awakening a renewed pride in the indigenous languages that were at risk of fading away.

And then, like a lightning strike illuminating the New Mexico sky, news of Mateo's achievements reached the hallowed halls of Harvard University. Recognizing the transformative impact of his work, Harvard awarded Mateo a scholarship to pursue Native American Studies—an opportunity that not only validated his efforts but elevated the cause of indigenous language preservation to a global platform.

As Mateo stands on the threshold of Harvard, he carries with him the hopes, stories, and languages of his people. His journey, fueled by action and guided by purpose, is a rallying call for students everywhere. In his own words, Mateo reflects, "The reservation is not just where I come from; it's the wellspring of my strength and the driving force behind my pursuit. Harvard is not just a destination; it's a platform to amplify the voices of indigenous cultures."

Mateo Rodriguez, the torchbearer of linguistic revitalization, invites every student to seize their dreams with action and purpose. His story echoes through the canyons of New Mexico, a testament to the transformative power of education and the unwavering commitment to preserving the cultural tapestry that makes us who we are. As Mateo steps onto the grounds of Harvard, he carries not just a scholarship but the promise of a future where indigenous languages thrive, resonate, and continue to tell the stories of generations past and those yet to come.

The Amazing Adventures of
MRGRANTMONEY

The Celestial Gala Chronicles: Mr. Grant Money's Odyssey to Cosmic Wisdom

*Step into the ethereal dreamscape where
Mr. Grant Money, adorned in celestial attire*

In the tapestry of dreams, Mr. Grant Money found himself immersed in a celestial reverie. As he drifted through the landscapes of slumber, the boundaries between reality and imagination blurred, giving rise to visions beyond the ordinary.

Within the dream's embrace, he stumbled upon an upscale celestial gala in the outer limits, a gathering of the brightest stars in human form. Cloaked in a celestial navy suit adorned with constellations and golden accents, Mr. Grant Money moved through the cosmic gathering, capturing the essence of a thousand galaxies.

In this ethereal dreamscape, a peculiar lizard approached him. Unbeknownst to Mr. Grant Money, it was Jerla in disguise, orchestrating another cosmic journey. As he reached to gently move the lizard away, a surge of energy enveloped him, transporting him to the outer limits, where celestial wisdom awaited.

In this celestial expanse, he encountered Hoosie, an elder spirit radiating wisdom and tranquility. A revelation unfolded – Hoosie was his grandpa, transformed into an elder spirit to guide and guard him on his cosmic adventures.

Hoosie's presence resonated with Mr. Grant Money, and a realization dawned upon him – his dream held cosmic insights. As Jerla whispered "consistency" into his left ear and gently touched his right, she revealed a three-month Scholarship Quest Consistency outline, a guide for students to gain and maintain momentum in their scholarship pursuits.

Clutching his Shirley Scepter and Golden Journal, Mr. Grant Money took note of every cosmic revelation. Swiftly, he sent a message to Maximus and Valencia, members of his Powerhouse Crew, instructing them to integrate this newfound wisdom into their online platform.

Boarding a cosmic vessel, scepter and journal in hand, Mr. Grant Money soared through the celestial expanse, wondering where his next venture would take him – somewhere to empower more victories and transform more lives. The celestial dream had not only unveiled cosmic wisdom but had also set the stage for the next chapter in the scholarship odyssey.

> "In the tapestry of dreams, I found a celestial gala in the outer limits, where stars in human form gathered. Cloaked in constellations, I moved through cosmic landscapes, capturing the essence of a thousand galaxies. Now, I carry that celestial wisdom to empower victories and transform lives. The scholarship odyssey continues!"
>
> - Mr. Grant Money

Exercise: "Scholarship Quest Consistency Outline"

Month 1: Discovery and Preparation

Week 1-2: Establish Your Foundation
- Research and list potential scholarships based on your academic goals, interests, and extracurricular activities.
- Create a master document to track scholarship details, requirements, and deadlines.

Week 3-4: Gather Essential Materials
- Update and polish your resume, highlighting academic achievements, extracurricular activities, and community involvement.
- Request letters of recommendation from teachers, mentors, or community leaders. Provide them with ample time and information.

Month 2: Crafting Stellar Applications

Week 1-2: Develop Your Personal Statement
- Reflect on your journey, experiences, and aspirations. Craft a compelling personal statement that showcases your uniqueness.
- Seek feedback from teachers, peers, or mentors to refine and enhance your narrative.

Week 3-4: Tailor Applications for Specific Scholarships
- Customize your applications for each scholarship, aligning them with the unique criteria and values of the awarding organization.
- Ensure your essays, transcripts, and letters of recommendation are tailored to each application.

Month 3: Submission and Follow-Up

Week 1-2: Polish and Proofread
- Review and refine your application materials, checking for grammatical errors, clarity, and coherence.
- Have a trusted mentor or teacher review your applications to provide additional feedback.

Week 3: Submit Applications
- Submit your scholarship applications well before the deadlines to avoid last-minute technical issues.
- Keep a checklist of submitted applications and confirmation emails.

Week 4: Follow-Up and Future Planning
- Send polite follow-up emails to confirm receipt of your applications.
- Use any downtime to research additional scholarships and start the preparation process for the next round.

Ongoing Strategies: Beyond the Three-Month Plan

- Stay engaged in extracurricular activities and community service to continually enhance your scholarship profile.
- Seek out new scholarship opportunities and add them to your master document.
- Regularly check in with teachers, mentors, or counselors for support and guidance.
- Embrace a mindset of continuous improvement, always looking for ways to strengthen your scholarship applications.

Consistency is key. By diligently following this three-month plan and maintaining an ongoing commitment to your scholarship journey, you pave the way for success in securing valuable financial aid for your educational pursuits. Good luck!

"In the cosmic expanse, I met Hoosie, my grandpa transformed into an elder spirit of wisdom. A revelation dawned – my dream held cosmic insights. With Shirley Scepter and Golden Journal, I unveil a three-month Scholarship Quest Consistency outline. Let's guide students to cosmic success, transcending the ordinary and reaching for the stars!"

- Mr. Grant Money

Discussion Questions

1. How does the celestial dreamscape in Mr. Grant Money's journey symbolize the intersection of imagination and reality, and how might this concept apply to our own lives and aspirations?

2. Explore the significance of the lizard, Jerla, in the story. How does the interaction with Jerla represent the unexpected catalysts or influencers that propel us into new realms of discovery and self-realization?

3. In the celestial expanse, Mr. Grant Money discovers that Hoosie, an elder spirit radiating wisdom, is his grandpa transformed. Discuss the symbolism behind this revelation and how ancestral connections or guidance can play a role in our personal and professional journeys.

4. Jerla imparts the word "consistency" to Mr. Grant Money, unveiling a three-month Scholarship Quest Consistency outline. How does this theme of consistency resonate throughout the story, and how can it be applied to one's pursuit of goals and aspirations in the real world?

5. Mr. Grant Money swiftly integrates the cosmic wisdom into his Powerhouse Crew's online platform. Discuss the theme of collaboration and shared knowledge in the story. How might collaborative efforts and the sharing of insights contribute to achieving individual and collective success in different aspects of life?

 Big Idea "Celestial Wisdom Scholarship Quest"

The Celestial Wisdom Scholarship Quest is a student-led initiative designed to help peers navigate the scholarship process with creativity and consistency. Inspired by the cosmos, the program includes a three-month "Scholarship Quest Plan" focused on researching opportunities, crafting stellar applications, and submitting them with confidence. Students can host cosmic-themed workshops like "Mapping Your Financial Galaxy" and create star-inspired vision boards to chart their goals. Alumni or community mentors act as guiding stars, sharing their scholarship success stories to inspire others. The initiative culminates in a celebratory showcase where students share wins and motivate others to reach for the stars in their educational journey.

🔍 Word Search

Embark on a cosmic journey with Mr. Grant Money as he navigates the celestial realms of dreams, uncovering secrets that hold the key to scholarship success. In this word search puzzle, delve into the tapestry of his ethereal adventures, discovering fifteen words intricately woven into the fabric of his celestial odyssey.

Can you find the hidden words that capture the essence of Mr. Grant Money's cosmic revelations?

Now, here are the 15 words for the word search puzzle based on the story:

T	P	R	I	E	C	E	I	I	L	T	M	T	N
C	I	E	P	C	O	C	C	O	I	R	A	L	O
O	H	M	D	E	N	L	O	I	G	A	W	O	R
S	S	O	R	L	S	S	N	E	R	N	I	D	R
M	R	N	E	E	T	L	S	A	A	Q	S	Y	E
I	A	E	A	S	E	C	I	M	N	U	D	S	V
C	L	Y	M	T	L	L	S	A	T	I	O	S	E
Y	O	A	S	I	L	I	T	Z	A	L	M	E	L
C	H	N	C	A	A	Z	E	Y	G	I	L	Y	A
I	C	E	A	L	T	A	N	R	G	T	C	A	T
S	S	A	P	E	I	R	C	Q	U	Y	L	L	I
A	L	R	E	J	O	D	Y	Y	T	A	G	C	O
V	I	D	S	I	N	R	A	L	G	O	O	A	N
G	N	E	A	T	S	I	C	M	E	O	N	E	I

TRANQUILITY
JERLA
REVELATION
CONSTELLATIONS
ODYSSEY
GRANT
LIZARD
SCHOLARSHIP
WISDOM
MONEY
COSMIC
CONSISTENCY
DREAMSCAPE
CELESTIAL
GALA

"In the celestial reverie, where dreams wove tales of cosmic wisdom, a peculiar lizard concealed Jerla's orchestration of another cosmic journey. As Mr. Grant Money embraced the ethereal dreamscape, Hoosie, an elder spirit, revealed himself as the grandpa guiding cosmic adventures.

SUCCESS STORIES

"Breaking the Genetic Code: Olivia Chang's Odyssey from Suburbia to Scientific Stardom"

In the quiet suburbs of Irvine, California, where manicured lawns mask the simmering potential of young minds, Olivia Chang embarked on a scientific odyssey that would challenge the very fabric of genetics. A tale of unraveling mysteries, breaking barriers, and earning a coveted scholarship to UC Berkeley—a journey that proves the microscopic can indeed be monumental.

Olivia's story begins with a tantalizing mystery—a question that echoed through the sterile hallways of suburban high school labs: Can a teenager, armed with curiosity and determination, make groundbreaking contributions to the realm of biotechnology? The answer, as Olivia would soon discover, was an emphatic yes.

In the seemingly ordinary community of Irvine, Olivia was anything but ordinary. A Chinese American student with a penchant for the microscopic, she delved into the intricate world of genetic engineering, navigating a landscape where few of her peers dared to tread. The challenges were as microscopic as the subjects of her research, but the triumphs, when uncovered, would reverberate far beyond the confines of suburban life.

Practically, Olivia's pursuit of her goal involved tireless hours in the lab—conducting experiments, analyzing data, and decoding the very language of genes. Her groundbreaking research in genetic engineering caught the attention of the scientific community, proving that age was no barrier to scientific achievement. Olivia wasn't just pushing the boundaries; she was rewriting the rules of what was deemed possible for a high school student.

The news of Olivia's achievements echoed through the academic corridors, reaching the discerning ears of UC Berkeley. The prestigious institution, known for its scientific prowess, recognized Olivia's potential and awarded her a scholarship to further her studies in biotechnology—a nod to her dedication in decoding the mysteries of our genetic makeup.

As Olivia prepares to make her mark at UC Berkeley, she reflects on the journey that led her from suburban labs to the forefront of genetic research. In a statement that encapsulates her spirit, Olivia shares, "In the world of genes, every discovery is a step toward unlocking the potential for a healthier, more sustainable future. UC Berkeley is not just a university; it's a canvas where I can paint the portrait of possibility in the language of DNA."

Olivia Chang's story is a captivating tale of a suburban scientist shattering preconceived notions and proving that scientific stardom knows no age. Her narrative invites every student, in suburbs or cities alike, to embrace their curiosity, challenge norms, and pursue their passions fearlessly. As she steps into the dynamic world of UC Berkeley, Olivia carries not just a scholarship but the promise of unraveling new genetic frontiers—one strand of DNA at a time.

AFTERWARD

As you reach the final pages of The Amazing Adventures of Mr. Grant Money, Volume 1, I hope you've been both entertained and enlightened by the captivating stories of our enigmatic protagonist, Mr. Grant Money. Through his remarkable adventures, you've explored the world of grants and philanthropy in an entirely new light.

These stories are not just tales of daring exploits and awe-inspiring achievements. They are also valuable lessons in grant acquisition, each with its unique insights and wisdom. However, the true magic happens when you put these lessons into practice. Remember, knowledge without action is like a locked treasure chest; it holds immense potential, but only when you open it does its true value become apparent.

It's important to recognize that in the world of grant acquisition, we all start at ground zero. What separates the triumphant from the rest is the determination to progress beyond that initial point. After reading these stories, take a moment to reflect on the lessons they impart and how you can apply them to your own journey in grant acquisition.

And there's no need to stop here! Mr. Grant Money's adventures continue with even more fascinating tales in Volumes 2 through 5. As you embark on these new journeys, embrace the valuable insights they offer. Keep in mind that knowledge, like a never-ending treasure trove, continues to expand. By continuing to learn and adapt, you too can achieve remarkable results in the world of grants and philanthropy.

If you're looking for further guidance and resources, consider visiting GrantCentralUSA.com and GrantAcquisition.com. These platforms offer a wealth of tools, courses, and expert advice to enhance your grant acquisition skills.

Remember, the key to success in grant acquisition is not just in learning but in applying what you've learned. As Mr. Grant Money has demonstrated, each adventure is an opportunity for growth, and your journey is no different. The power to make a difference in your community and beyond is within your grasp.

So, gear up for the next volumes of Mr. Grant Money's incredible adventures, and keep striving to transform your grant acquisition endeavors into triumphant tales of your own. Your journey is just beginning, and there's no limit to what you can achieve. The world of grants and philanthropy is waiting for your story to unfold, and the possibilities are limitless.

ABOUT THE AUTHOR

Rodney Walker is a man on a mission. He's dedicated his life to helping others secure funding for their projects and dreams. As the President of Grant Central USA, a grant development training firm internationally known for helping organizations land six-figure and seven-figure grants and shave months off the time it takes to get funded, Rodney has helped clients raise over half a billion dollars in grants!

He's also an author of numerous books, online courses and the founder of two popular grant writing conferences: The Education Grants Conference and First Responders Grants Conference. Grant Central USA has also partnered with several universities, including Regis University, Hawaii University, Oklahoma University, National University, Cal Poly University, and Florida Atlantic University.

Rodney is even the host of four podcasts: Get Funded with Rodney, Grant Writing Today, Grant Business Show, and Schools Winning Grants. He oversees Grant Success Advisors, an elite network of approved licensees who deliver today's leading training in grant development systems.

He has an extensive network of high-level contacts, including his Grant Writers Association group on Linkedin with over 15,000+ members.

Considered a national authority in the grant industry, Grant Central USA's clients have included, The Magic Johnson Foundation, the George W. Bush Foundation, Ben Guillory and Danny Glover of the Robey Theatre Company, Hawaii State Teachers Association, United Way, Habitat for Humanity, and numerous school districts and city governments.

Rodney has produced over 730 videos on grant development on his popular YouTube channel and has taught over 240,000 people how to improve their grant writing efforts. "We have been helping our clients successfully get funded and launch new careers in grant writing since 2006 across the U.S. and worldwide, giving them both the competence and the confidence to win the grants at a high level."

He says his primary specialty is "Getting our clients funded with six-figure and seven-figure grants while helping grant professionals get paid what they are worth!"

In addition to his leadership experience at Grant Central USA, he has years of experience in Business and Professional Development in various sectors. He has been a sought-after expert in grant professional development, coaching, and the law of success.

As a media personality, he has interviewed numerous celebrities, including Snoop Dogg, Heisman Trophy Winners: Reggie Bush, Charles Woodson, Professional Boxer Laila Ali, America's Next Top Model Season 19 Winner: Laura James, NBA Champions: Draymond Green, Matt Barnes, National College Football Champions: Coach Mack Brown, and Vince Young, and countless others.

It's safe to say that Rodney knows his stuff regarding grants and working with champions!

MGM Music to Get You Going 🎷 and 🎶 Keep You Soaring!

Music has the power to make life and learning more joyful. Get ready to have a blast with Mr. Grant Money Music, where every tune is fun, upbeat, and filled with positivity. These story-driven songs not only entertain but also educate and inspire, making your journey both enjoyable and enriching. 🎶

Dive into a symphony of stories and inspiration with Mr. Grant Money Music, where every note is a step toward greater success.

You can enjoy Mr. Grant Money Music on most major streaming platforms, including Spotify, Apple Music, and Amazon Music, bringing inspiration and positivity right to your favorite device. 🎧

Diverse Musical Flavors to Satisfy Every Listening Craving

Topical and Seasonal Themes

Enjoy our themed musical sessions that align with the seasons and current events, offering fresh perspectives and innovative ideas from today's Top Master Grant Acquisition Specialist, Mr. Grant Money!

Experience Our Other Dynamic Series with Mr. Grant Money!

Harvesting Hope: The Global Odyssey of Mr. Grant Money

Vol. 1

ISBN 978-0-9659275-0-5

The Artful Navigator: Mr. Grant Money's Chronicles

Vol. 2

ISBN 978-0-9659275-2-9

Grantopoly: Mr. Grant Money's Out-of-This-World Wisdom

Vol. 3

ISBN 978-0-9659275-3-6

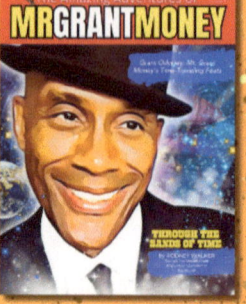

Grant Odyssey: Mr. Grant Money's Time-Traveling Feats

Vol. 4

ISBN 978-0-9659275-4-3

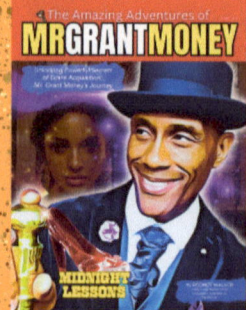

Unlocking Powerful Secrets of Grant Acquisition

Vol. 5

ISBN 978-0-9659275-5-0

The Entrepreneurial Classroom: Teens Redefining Success

Vol. 1

ISBN 979-8-89725-005-9

Mindset Mastery: Developing The Teen Entrepreneurial Spirit

Vol. 2

ISBN 979-8-89725-006-6

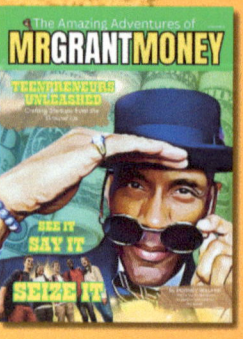

Teenpreneurs Unleashed: Crafting Startups From The Ground Up

Vol. 3

ISBN 979-8-89725-007-3

Business Battlefront: Teens Conquering Challenges In Startups

Vol. 4

ISBN 979-8-89725-008-0

Teen Changemakers: Social Impact Entrepreneurship in Action

Vol. 5

ISBN 979-8-89725-009-7

Pocket Power: A Guide to Practical Budgeting for Teens

Vol. 1

ISBN 979-8-89725-010-3

Fortune Foundations: Navigating Tomorrow's Savings Landscape

Vol. 2

ISBN 979-8-89725-011-0

Profit Pioneers: Young Entrepreneurs Unleashed

Vol. 3

ISBN 979-8-89725-012-7

Scholarly Cents: A College Finance Expedition

Vol. 4

ISBN 979-8-89725-013-4

Financial Fortitude: Navigating Life's Financial Storm

Vol. 5

ISBN 979-8-89725-014-1

Win More Scholarship In Less Time with These...

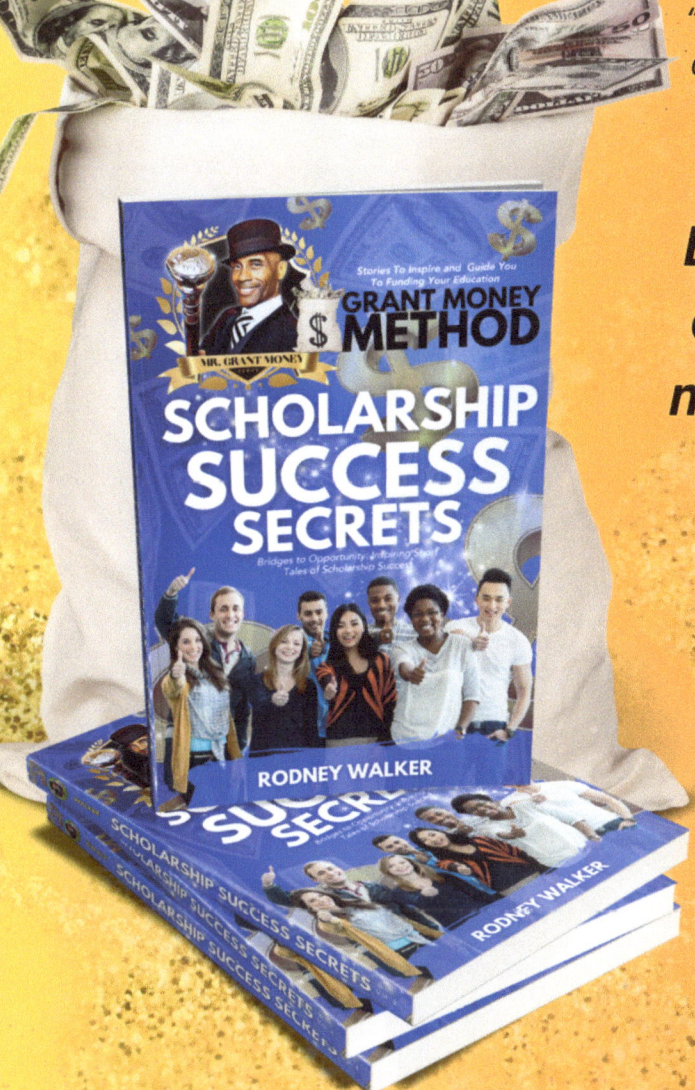

"Thank you so much for your help. Probably not a day has gone by that I didn't use something."
- Evelyn Barker, Director of Grants and Special Project at University of Texas

Elevate your scholarship efforts into success with my proven strategies that have raised millions.

Scholarship Success Secret is not just a guide; it's a storytelling journey like no other. Across five compelling books, Mr. Grant Money—takes you into the lives of students, parents, and educators.

Through these vivid, relatable tales, you'll uncover the insider secrets, proven strategies, and practical steps to secure the scholarships and education grants you need for college and beyond.

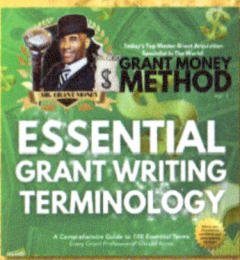

Boost your confidence in grant writing, fundraising, and finance! Elevate your communication skills with the **Fundraising Fundamentals Vocabulary Builder Series** – *100 essential terms in each series.* Invest in knowledge, empower your success!

Enjoy More Amazing Adventures with Mr. Grant Money!

Scholarship Odyssey:
Mr. Grant Money's Roadmap

Vol. 1

ISBN 979-8-89725-000-4

Journey To Acceptance:
Navigating College Applications

Vol. 2

ISBN 979-8-89725-001-1

Passion Into Practice:
Specialized Scholarship

Vol. 3

ISBN 979-8-89725-002-8

Passport To Success:
Navigating Global Scholarships

Vol. 4

ISBN 979-8-89725-003-5

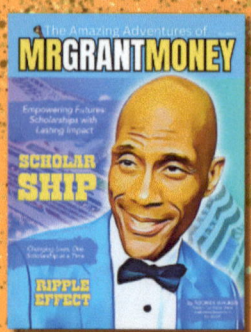

Empowering Futures:
Scholarships With Lasting Impact

Vol. 5

ISBN 979-8-89725-004-2

Gain Exclusive Access To Companion Resources & Bonus Materials at MrGrantMoney.com and GrantCentralUsa.com

LICENSED

Bring the transformative Adventures and lessons of Mr. Grant Money to your educational institution or organization by **acquiring your license today**. Enjoy exclusive access to a wealth of online resources, such as special reports, worksheets, videos, audio training, discounts, and more, elevating the entire experience to the next level!

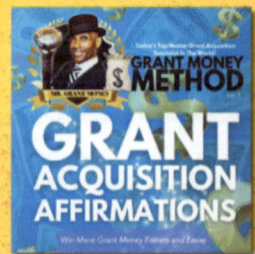

Envision and affirm your grant success in the same proactive spirit as Mr. Grant Money. **Experience the power of these daily affirmations** to inspire and motivate your journey toward success!